For Their Sake

For Their Sake

Recognizing,
Responding to,
and Reporting
CHILD ABUSE

Becca Cowan Johnson

For Kids Sake, Inc.

American Camping Association ®

Published by American Camping Association, Inc.
Printed in the United States of America

American Camping Association
5000 State Road 67 North
Martinsville, IN 46151-7902

American Camping Association National Office
317/342-8456

American Camping Association Bookstore
800/428-CAMP

FAX
317/342-2065

Library of Congress Cataloging-in-Publication Data

Johnson, Becca Cowan, 1954–
    For their sake : recognizing, responding to, and
reporting child abuse / Becca Cowan Johnson, with
For Kids Sake, Inc.
        p.   cm.
    Includes bibliographic references and index.
    ISBN 0-87603-128-9
    1. Child abuse—United States—Investigation—
Handbooks, manuals, etc. 2. Child abuse—Reporting—
United States—Handbooks, manuals, etc. 3. Child care
workers—United States—Handbooks, manuals, etc.
I. For Kids Sake, Inc. II. Title.
HV8079.C46J64 1992
363.2'595554—dc20   91-43349
                                              CIP

Table of Contents

Acknowledgements   x
About the Authors   xi

Part I   **Understanding Abuse**   1

One   *The Importance of Involvement*   3

Why Should You Read This Book?   3
The Prevalence of Child Abuse   4
Responses to Child Abuse   6
Why Become Involved?   6
Responsibility   9

Two   *Historical Perspective*   11

The Beginnings of Child Abuse   12
The Nineteenth Century   13
Child Abuse Today   14

Three   *Types of Abuse*   17

Physical Abuse   18
Neglect   20

Sexual Abuse | 22
Emotional Abuse | 24
Additional Abuse Situations | 26

Four **_Causes of Abuse_** **31**

Background Indicators | 31
Situational Factors | 33
Personality Factors | 35

Five **_Indicators of Abuse_** **39**

Indicators of Sexual Abuse | 40
Indicators of Neglect | 41
Indicators of Emotional Abuse | 42
Indicators of Physical Abuse | 43
Physical Abuse Described—Wound Identification | 44
Wound Identification Summary | 50

Six **_Reporting Requirements_** **53**

Reporting Facts and Responsibilities | 53
Acknowledging Reporting Requirements | 55
Reporting Concerns and Questions | 56
Reporting Laws | 60

Part II **Working with Abuse Victims** **63**

Seven **_What to Do When You Suspect or Discover Child Abuse_** **65**

Youth Service Organizations Are Often
 the First to Know | 65
What to Do and What to Report | 67
Reporting—Again | 73

Eight   ***Abuse Accusations—Truth or Consequences***   75

Why Most Accusations Are True   77
Why Many False Accusations Are Revealing   79
Why Some Accusations Are False   80
When in Doubt, Report   81

Nine   ***Reactions to Abuse***   83

Reactions to Abuse   83
Feelings About Abuse   85
Questions Victims Ask   87
Possible Outcomes of Abuse   88

Ten   ***Working with Abuse Victims***   93

Practical Suggestions   94
Be A Child Advocate   98
Programs for the Abused   98

Part III Working with Staff Members   101

Eleven   ***Staff Screening and Selection— Abuser Characteristics***   103

General Characteristics of Potential Abusers   103
Characteristics of the Potential Physical
   and Emotional Abuser   104
Characteristics of the Potential Sexual Abuser   106
Sex Offenders   107

Twelve   ***Staff Selection—The Application, Interview, and References***   115

The Application   115
The Interview   116
Interview Questions   118
References   119

Thirteen *Staff Training*   121

    Commitment   122
    Guidelines for Staff Training   122
    Training Outline 1   124
    Training Outline 2—Short Version   126
    How to Present   127

Fourteen *Precautions and Prevention*   129

    For Those in Charge—Precautions and Preventions 129
    For Staff Members—Precautions and Preventions   132
    For Children—Prevention Ideas
        and Skills   136

Fifteen *Documentation—A Safeguard*   139

    Document Policies and Procedures   140
    Documentation of Incidents, Observations,
        and Responsibilities   143

Sixteen *Summary*   149

    Reminders and Suggestions   149

Part IV **Reference Materials**   151

    Cited Reference List   153

    Suggested Reading List   155

    Appendices   159

    A. Sample Mandated Reporter
        Acknowledgement Form   161
    B. Sample Child Abuse Law (Massachusetts) 164
    C. Sample Child Abuse Report Form (California) 168
    D. Audio-Visual Resources   170
    E. Organizational and Support-Group Resources 173

F. Sample Staff Application Form   175
G. Sample Authorization to Check Criminal
        Record   177
H. Case Histories   178
I. Child Abuse Prevention Information
        for Children   181
    Prevention List   181
    Alert List   183
J. Sample Accident/Incident Report Form   185
K. Sample Incident Report Form   187
L. Sample Information Supplement Form
        for Reporting   188
M. Sample Visual Supplement Form
        for Reporting   190
N. Checklist of Possible Indicators of Abuse   191
O. Sample Health Screening Forms   194
P. The Effects of Abuse at Different
        Developmental Stages   197
Q. Child Abuse Information—Treatment,
        Intervention, Education   200

Index   201

Acknowledgements

I would like to thank the staff of the Parents Center in Santa Cruz, California, for their dedicated example in providing counseling services for abuse victims. The training and experience I gained there were invaluable.

I would like to thank those who assisted in the development of this book: to my mother, Avis Cowan and my friend, Alison Short Miles for assistance in editing the first draft of this book; to Joan and Bryan Harmelink for the use of their facilities when writing this book; to Marge Scanlin, Ph.D. for recommendations and revisions; and to Grechen Perry Throop for encouragement; and to other ACA staff for their assistance in making this book happen.

Thank you to the many people who shared their stories and allowed me to participate in their recovery. This book is dedicated to them and to those whose stories have yet to be revealed.

About the Authors

Becca Cowan Johnson

Becca Cowan Johnson obtained a Ph.D. from the University of Southern California counseling in educational psychology (with an emphasis in developmental psychology and child development). She has also received postdoctoral training and licensure in clinical psychology. Johnson has worked with victims of abuse and their families, and has conducted staff training seminars on child abuse for agencies that provide programs and services for children and adolescents. She received her master's degree in recreation administration and is a certified camp director with the American Camping Association. Johnson has worked with children and adolescents in a variety of settings (recreational, day care, camp, and counseling/therapy).

For Kids Sake, Inc.

For Kids Sake, Inc., is an international not-for-profit, privately funded agency dedicated to the prevention of child abuse through education and intervention. The organization was founded in 1974 by the James Mead family.

The Meads' dedication to the prevention of child abuse and the organization began with their efforts to prevent an abused girl from being placed in a mental institution. They succeeded. Today, that child and six other victims of child abuse live with the Meads.

For Kids Sake strives to serve all who need help: children,

parents, and families. The organization currently offers, publications, and videos; child-abuse prevention programs; and professional training and education for doctors, nurses, therapists, law-enforcement officers, district attorneys, teachers, church leaders, and other professionals—in fact, For Kids Sake trains more than 100,000 people each year.

James Mead, the organizaton's founder and president, is an internationally recognized expert on child abuse, molestation, parent education, and law enforcement strategies. He has written numerous articles, four books, and a training manual on child abuse. He serves as a special consultant to many national police, child-protective, and corrections departments and agencies.

David Westgate, the executive director, has presented training seminars nationally for law-enforcement personnel, teachers, and medical professionals. He served on a committee of the California Commission on Peace Officers Standards and Training that revised guidelines on investigating child abuse in that state.

PART I

Understanding Abuse

▶ An overview of the prevalence, historical background, types, causes, indicators, and reporting requirements of abuse.

The Importance of Involvement

"*I* thought I knew enough about the child-abuse reporting requirements," a youth worker shared, "but when I had to deal with a situation first hand, I realized how much I didn't know and how much I needed to know."

As one who works with young people, you play a significant role in the enhancement of children's lives. The nature of your work centers on helping children enjoy and learn from life; at the same time, you provide them care and protection. It is, therefore, important that you be well-informed regarding child-abuse issues as you strive to provide quality service to your clientele.

Why Should You Read This Book?

This book was written for those who provide programs and services for children and adolescents. Special concerns that exist in these work settings necessitate your having specific information about child abuse. Whether the program or service is a residential or day camp, a recreational program, a club activity, day care, a church youth program, or after-school supervision, people providing those and other services need to know about child abuse and about their specific responsibilities. The caring, enjoyable environment these activities and organizations afford, along with the ongoing contact with children and youth, enhances the possibility of discovering or suspecting child abuse.

This book is written for the following kinds of people:

Recreational staff—May be from government departments (municipal, county, or state recreational programs) as well as from service agencies such as Girl Scouts, Boy Scouts, Camp Fire, Girls/Boys Clubs, YMCA, YWCA, church youth programs, and others. Staff members, paid or volunteer, may serve as supervisors, directors, superintendents, program directors, recreation or club leaders, activity instructors, and aides. Services may be provided daily (such as after-school care and playground supervision), weekly (club meetings, youth groups, and recreational classes), or as scheduled (special events and outings).

Camp staff members—Work in both resident and day camps, whether church, agency, or privately sponsored. Program-oriented camp staff members include directors, program directors, counselors, unit leaders, and activity instructors. Operational or support staff positions encompass those in food service, maintenance, administration, and health care (camp nurse). In the camp setting, the operational staff as well as the program staff should receive training in child-abuse issues, due to the fact that most employees have at least some contact with campers regardless of their job responsibilities.

Child-care workers—Encompass all of those providing child-care services, such as before- and after-school supervision, preschool learning opportunities, and child care. These may include agency, church, and municipally or privately owned facilities, as well as licensed home care and babysitting services. Positions include director, teacher, worker, activity leader, and provider.

Others—All workers and organizations providing programs and/or services for minors.

The Prevalence of Child Abuse

Studies have revealed startling statistics regarding the number of abused children. In a study conducted among 1,800 college students, one-third of the female participants and one-third of the male participants reported having been subjected to some form of sexual abuse as children. Only half the females and one-tenth of the males citing such experiences had ever reported it to their parents.

In *The Secret Trauma* (1986), Diana Russell cites findings on the prevalence of child sexual abuse of females. She reports that of nine-hundred and thirty women surveyed thirty-eight percent responded that they had been victims of incestuous and/or extra-familial abuse prior to age eighteen. When the definition of sexual abuse was broadened to include non-contact experiences such as exhibitionism and sexual advance, fifty-four percent responded that they had been victims. This means that approximately one in every two women has had some undesired sexual encounter.

In another study, Russell found that one of every three females is sexually assaulted before her eighteenth birthday. Finkelhor (1984) found that one of every seven boys experienced some form of sexual abuse before the age of eighteen. Finkelhor's study also indicated that one-fourth of all abuse occurs to children under the age of seven.

The California State Department of Social Service (Statistical Services Branch) reported nearly 140,000 cases of child abuse in 1984. Physical abuse was a factor in 29.3 percent of those cases; sexual abuse was a factor in 18.8 percent; neglect was a factor in 35.5 percent; and emotional abuse was a factor in 3.3 percent of the cases.

The Massachusetts Department of Social Services reported that of the abuse cases reported in 1985, neglect was a factor in fifty-two percent, physical abuse was a factor in thirty-four percent, and sexual abuse was a factor in fourteen percent. The department further reported that children ages five to twelve are at the greatest risk of sexual abuse. Of the substantiated reports twenty-five percent involved children five years of age and under; forty-two percent, children five to twelve years of age; and thirty-three percent, children between twelve and eighteen years old.

For Kids Sake, Inc. states that reported statistics represent only the tip of the iceberg. Current reports indicate that there are a minimum of two million children abused or neglected each year, including five thousand deaths due to child abuse.

Responses to Child Abuse

Some people whose jobs bring them in contact with children would like to ignore the problem of child abuse in the hope that it will go away. These people either do not understand their legal responsibilities or the physical and emotional harm that come to an abused child.

After a class session that covered the legal reporting responsibilities regarding abuse, as well as some of the ways to recognize it, a student of mine asked for advice. She worked part-time at a child-care center and discovered that one of the children had several visible bruises. The student remembered the class presentation on injuries and possible explanations and felt that these bruises were suspicious in nature. When asked, the child was unable to adequately explain the marks and became unusually withdrawn and sad. The student knew that she must report the situation, but when she told the center's director, she was told, "It's probably not abuse and not that bad. I don't want us to get involved; it might cause repercussions."

While some people, like the center's director, try to ignore the existence of child abuse, others become overwhelmed by the prevalence of this unfortunate societal problem. This causes them to become apathetic and inactive, and their passivity conveys an "I'm only one person. What could I do anyway?" attitude.

There are others, however, who are aware of their social, moral, and legal obligations. These people strive to be informed with regards to recognizing, responding to, and reporting child abuse in an effort to contribute to its deterrence. In reading this book, you are joining this group of people who seek to help by actively becoming more aware of what they can and must do.

Why Become Involved?

For the Child

The foremost reason to become actively involved in both the reporting and prevention of child abuse is to protect children. Abuse leaves visible as well as invisible scars that follow them into adulthood. The emotional and physical pain inflicted go far beyond the abusive encounters.

Those working with children need to be advocates for their safety. Whether working with children in a recreation, camp, or child-care setting, the safety of each child is of utmost importance. By keeping first-aid kits nearby, fire extinguishers in strategic places, and emergency phone numbers readily accessible, we prepare ourselves to act in the event of an *accident*. Yet we are generally ill-prepared to handle *incidents* of abuse, even though we are in key positions to detect it.

For the Family

Some people feel hesitant to report suspected abusive situations, knowing the possible trauma it may cause the affected family. They do not want to cause additional pain or bring shame upon the family or to be blamed for doing so, especially if they know the family.

Many people find it easier to become involved and help the family through the discovery and investigation process if the alleged abuser is not a member of the immediate family. If the alleged abuser is a family member, however, the worker often struggles with the need to report the situation.

During a summer family camp, a counselor asked to speak with me about a situation involving a camper in his group. The teenage camper shared with the counselor information about his physically and emotionally abusive father. He told the counselor about numerous times when his father had beaten him, causing bruises and cuts; on one occasion, his injuries necessitated medical attention. The counselor knew the father, who lived in the same area. He wanted to talk with the father and make him realize the emotional and physical harm he was causing his son. The counselor had hopes of helping by confronting the father and offering to assist in whatever ways were possible because he lived nearby.

In his desire to help, however, the counselor did not realize that he potentially would be causing much greater danger for the boy. Quite possibly, the father's abusive behavior would escalate because his son had revealed the abuse. I reminded the counselor that his role was to report what he had been told and to leave the rest in the hands of the child-welfare-agency professionals. *The sooner professional involvement is obtained through reporting, the sooner the child will receive greater protection from harm.*

One of the best ways we can help an abusive family is to let the situation come out into the open. This not only provides protection for the abused person, but also forces the family to admit their need to get professional help for the problem. In seeking to deal with the situation ourselves, we inappropriately take on the roles of rescuer, judge, and professional therapist.

For State Reporting Requirements

Whether or not you are interested in learning more about this tragic societal problem, state laws mandate that you be actively involved. Those whose jobs bring them into contact with children are obligated to be informed about child abuse and about the requirement of reporting known or suspected abuse incidents. It is not optional.

We become involved because we are required to do so, but hopefully, we become involved because we care about children. After all, isn't that why we do what we do?

For Your Protection Against Accusations

Another important reason for those working with young people to become aware of child abuse is for their own protection. If staff members are carefully selected and trained, the possibility of problems and accusations against the agency, organization, or one of the staff members may be minimized. Accusations, whether true or false, have quickly closed the doors of many programs and agencies that were not educated in recognizing, responding to, and reporting child abuse. They were not prepared.

Responsibility

My student recounted her second attempt at informing the child-care-center director about the child's unexplained injuries. After hearing her concerns about the safety of the child, the director not only refused to get involved, but also threatened to fire the student if she were to report the "unlikely" abuse.

This student felt confused and feared losing her job. After all, she was a child-development major at the university and hoped to operate a preschool one day. I reviewed the child-abuse reporting responsibilities with her before asking, "According to the law, is the director required to report something like this? If so, what must you do if she refuses?" She answered, "I know that she is supposed to report, and if she doesn't, I must do it."

She hesitated only briefly before continuing, "But even if I were not required to report, I would do it anyway—for the child's sake."

Historical Perspective

*A*s previously stated, there are more than two million cases of serious abuse reported every year in the United States. These reports of abuse are not limited to any particular group of people or geographic location in our society. If they were, perhaps abusive situations would be easier to detect and to prevent.

Abuse is considered to be "unbiased" with regard to ethnicity, socioeconomic status, geographic locale, religious beliefs, and age of the perpetrator. That is, abuse occurs in all cultural and ethnic groups, at all age levels, among a variety of occupational and religious groups, and within all income levels.

With regard to gender, however, sexual abuse does have some specialized statistics. Most abusers (perpetrators) are males, often trusted adults or relatives of their victims. Female sexual-abuse victims greatly outnumber reported male victims—seventy-one percent of all reported sexually abused children are female. (Note: This possibly is due to the fact that male victims are much less likely to report the abuse.) Interestingly, however, one survey reported that when all types of maltreatment (sexual, physical and emotional abuse, and neglect) were considered together, the percentage of male and female victims was approximately equal.

It is ironic that we tell children to be wary of strangers, since most abusers are known by the child. We neglect to inform children what they should do in the event that the abusive person is a family member, family friend, babysitter, teacher, coach, or neighbor.

Child rearing has traditionally been a private family matter. In our society, parents and other family members have cared for and disciplined their children in the manner they saw fit, with a minimum of outside interference. Times have changed, however, and growing awareness of the incidence and degree of child mistreatment is altering the public's attitude toward child-rearing practices. There is increasing concern that children must be protected from harm regardless of its source.

The Beginnings of Child Abuse

Child abuse is a serious problem that dates back as far as recorded history. Over the centuries, children have been killed, abandoned, neglected, and cruelly chastised. Despite this, the maltreatment of children by their parents has aroused public concern only in recent times. The motives for killing and abusing children are many. The practice of infanticide—the killing of newborn babies by drowning, suffocation, exposure to the elements, or abandonment—has recurred throughout history for many reasons and, unfortunately, still occurs today.

Until the twentieth century, children were considered to be property; parents could do with them as they pleased. In ancient Rome, a man could sell, abandon, or kill his child and still remain within the norms of society. The rights of the father included the right to sell his children into slavery; often, daughters were sold as prostitutes.

Ancient philosophers, Biblical writers, and American colonists believed that sparing the rod spoiled the child. The maltreatment of children was justified for centuries by the belief that severe physical punishment was necessary to maintain discipline, to transmit educational ideas, to please certain gods, or to expel evil spirits. Beatings to drive out evil were a form of psychiatric treatment especially applicable to children. In cultures where epilepsy was attributed to demonic possession, the sufferer was soundly thrashed to expel the demon. In India, a sacred iron chain was used expressly for this purpose. American colonists, with their great devotion to religious beliefs, enacted laws that demanded obedience from children.

The Nineteenth Century

Even during the nineteenth century, economic exploitation of children occurred. Children were sometimes forced to labor in mines and sweatshops in Great Britain. They were chained to their posts and whipped by their overseers to ensure that they would work for long hours.

In addition, children were fed very little. Parents felt that they could get some use out of their troublesome offspring by working them to death. The parents received the income that the child earned, using it to support the family. Once the child died, the additional income would be eliminated, but so, too, would be the one who created the need.

North America—New York Foundling Hospital

Child abandonment and infanticide had reached a crisis point. Children were being discarded in gutters and garbage cans. The most stirring plea for action against abuse was made by Archbishop John McClosky. It was the Sisters of Charity of New York City who accepted the challenge of saving these unwanted babies.

The Sisters set up the New York Foundling Hospital in a small brownstone building at 17 East 12th Street. It opened its doors on October 11, 1869, in the hope that desperate mothers would choose to abandon their unwanted babies in a safe place rather than in gutters or garbage cans. A crib was placed in front of the hospital so that babies could be placed in it anonymously.

Within a few months, the N.Y. Foundling Hospital was overflowing with unwanted infants. The objective had been realized; proof of that was the downward trend of infanticide. Several other large cities in the United States began to set up their own foundling homes.

The Society for the Prevention of Cruelty to Children

Although public opinion was changing, the first case to establish a precedent for children's rights did not occur until 1874 in New York. The case involved a girl, approximately ten years of age, who had been neglected and physically abused by her adoptive mother. Her body showed signs of having been beaten frequently. Not a single government body was willing to handle the case in court, so Henry Bergh, the founder of the Society for the Prevention of Cruelty to Animals, initiated a petition whereby a special warrant was issued to bring the child before the court. The child was placed elsewhere temporarily (exactly where is unknown) for seven months, pending efforts to locate her relatives. When none could be found, she was committed to the Sheltering Arms, an orphan asylum.

On April 7, 1874, the mother was prosecuted under indictments for felonious assault with a pair of scissors and for a series of assaults during 1873 and 1874. The jury found her guilty of assault and battery and sentenced her to one year of hard labor in a penitentiary. As a result of this case, the Society for the Prevention of Cruelty to Children was organized in New York in 1874.

By 1889, thirty-one such societies in Great Britain had united to form the National Society for the Prevention of Cruelty to Children, with Queen Victoria as its patron. Also, Parliament passed an act for the prevention of cruelty to children, dubbed "The Children's Charter."

Child Abuse Today

There are still countries where children may be beaten and mutilated, where desperate mothers murder or throw away their infants, and where it is common to destroy physically handicapped children. The methods used in infanticide have not changed much throughout history. Blood is rarely shed; head trauma, strangulation, and drowning are the most common methods.

Abuse and neglect occur in all classes and cultures where economic instability, unprepared parents, social stress and isolation, parental self-hate, a misdirected sex drive, and/or the inability to cope with the pressures of everyday life exist. It is important to understand that any person has the potential to abuse or neglect a child, given the necessary combination of circumstances. Abuse and molestation are committed by upset, frustrated adults, not just by those who are considered to be mentally ill.

A child who is physically, sexually, or mentally tortured and for whom no one intervenes, most likely will be scarred emotionally for life—if he or she survives. Depending on the type and severity of the abuse and/or neglect, long-term physical effects can include mental retardation; the loss of hearing, sight, or speech; and the lessening of motor skills. Victims may also suffer learning and behavioral disorders. Their emotional needs sometimes seem to be insatiable. Many are destined to pattern their own parenting after their upbringing, becoming abusers of their own children perpetuating what is known as the *cycle of abuse*.

Unfortunately, most cases of child abuse go unreported. In 1973, the approximate nationwide reporting rate was estimated at 350 reports per million population in the United States. This rate produces a figure of more than seventy thousand reports for the year. Only eleven years later, in 1984, more child-abuse cases were reported in Los Angeles County alone than were thought to occur in the entire nation ten years earlier.

Many people feel that the maltreatment of children is a thing of the past. They tend either to ignore the problem or refuse to believe the prevalence of it. Yet it is a very real problem of the present, a problem that needs focused attention and dedicated people to educate society in an effort to help curb the incidence and pain of child abuse.

Types of Abuse

*G*enerally, when we talk about child abuse, we are referring to any maltreatment of a minor. Unfortunately, what one person may consider maltreatment, another may consider appropriate discipline. An abusive act is one in which physical and/or emotional harm occurs.

The Federal Child Abuse Prevention and Treatment Act provides this definition: "Child abuse and neglect means the physical or mental injury, sexual abuse or exploitation, negligent treatment, or maltreatment of a child under the age of eighteen."

An acquaintance asked me for advice regarding a friend of his. He had observed a mark on the friend's child and discovered that the child had been struck by the parent. When he confronted his friend, the parent admitted that she had been stressed out and lost control. The parent further claimed that this had happened only one other time.

Child abuse is usually not an isolated event but a pattern of behavior that an adult uses in interacting with a child. This behavior generally increases in severity and frequency and may be exhibited on a regular or sporadic basis. Even if marks were not visible on other occasions, it is likely that the negative pattern of interacting with the child is an ongoing behavior. That is, the probability is high that additional physical as well as emotional abuse is occurring in the friend's home.

When we talk about child abuse, we generally are referring to one of the four types or categories listed below. These are explained in this chapter. Types of abuse include:

1. Physical abuse
2. Neglect (physical and/or emotional)
3. Sexual abuse
4. Emotional abuse

Physical Abuse

Physical abuse is one of the most commonly identified forms of abuse due to the physical trauma. It occurs when someone inflicts bodily harm that leaves a physical injury. Visible external injuries include bruises, burns, black eyes, and cuts.

Not all physical injuries, however, are visible. Internal injuries, head trauma, and broken bones resulting from an abusive encounter may go unnoticed.

Important in the identification of physical trauma is the comparison of the child's injuries with the explanation given for them, either by the child or the caretaker. Adults attempt to avoid detection by devising all kinds of explanations that they hope will be accepted as the cause of the injuries.

Many who work in people-oriented jobs want to believe people, giving them the benefit of the doubt. It is hard to accept the possibility of abuse, especially in a family that you know. But a careful review of wound patterns often will produce a clearer picture of what really happened to the child in light of the explanation given.

In one case, a seven-year-old boy was observed to have multiple straight-line lacerations on his back. A report was filed with the local authorities, and an investigation was begun. The parent's explanation was that while the children were roughhousing, the seven-year-old fell over backward onto a stack of books and that the edges of the books caused the injuries. The child told the same story and refused to implicate anyone.

During the investigation, a souvenir baseball bat was found at the home. The investigator adjusted a dress form to the size of the child and draped it with white muslin. Next, he took the bat and placed it in a bag containing blue carpenter's chalk, shaking the bag so that the chalk coated the toy bat. Then, he repeatedly struck the mannequin with the bat to re-create the injury pattern. The pattern of blue chalk was photographed and compared with the one taken of the child after the injury occurred. Both photos were shown to the parent and to the child, who subsequently admitted that the re-creation was correct.

Wound identification and possible behavioral indicators of physical abuse are discussed further in chapter five.

Physical Abuse or Accidental Injury

Usually, the nature and type of the injury provide consistent clues as to whether it was incurred by accident. Considering the age of the child, investigators can determine what accidents might cause specific bruises, burns, cuts, lacerations, and other injuries.

Many times, those who work with young people neglect a simple screening technique that can help to determine whether a noted injury was the result of an accident or of abuse. Much can be gained by taking a genuine interest in the child, showing care and concern, and asking about the physical injury.

Generally, the child will give either of two types of responses. The first response is to recount an exciting story that the child will want to tell, demonstrating an accidental injury. For example, when asked, Susie might answer, "I was racing down the street on my new bicycle and came around the corner too fast. I ran into a tree and fell off the bike."

The second type of response is characterized by a hesitant answer from the child. The story may seem inconsistent with the injuries sustained, and the child may not want to answer. For example, when asked, Jimmy tells you that he doesn't remember how he got the cuts and bruises on his arm. What actually happened was that his father threw him against the wall in anger.

This simple screening technique can reveal much.

Neglect

Neglect occurs when parents or guardians fail to provide for the child. Most reported neglect cases involve lack of proper food, shelter, clothing, medical care, and supervision. Some neglect is a result of ignorance of proper child care; other forms of neglect involve deliberate maltreatment of the minor.

One example of neglect occurred with a young mother who had no education and no experience with children. When her child became ill with a high fever, she placed the girl in a closet because she had heard that children sometimes go blind when they have high fevers. After a week in the closet, the child finally recovered from the fever, but she was left with permanent brain damage.

Neglect is considered to be a form of child abuse, but in many ways, it is a separate problem. It may be a single problem, such as lack of supervision or lack of proper food or clothing, but usually is a combination of several neglectful behaviors. In many cases, homes in which neglect occurs are not necessarily abusive—just severely lacking in quality.

Physical neglect is not limited to families with little money, it even occurs in families with adequate financial resources. In these situations, the parents neglect to provide necessities for the child while actively supporting their own needs.

Not all neglect is physical; there is also emotional neglect. In homes where this occurs, the parents provide the child with physical necessities (food, clothing, shelter, and medical care) but give little or no emotional support. The parents seemingly ignore the child and his or her need for nurturing.

Some of the more commonly identified types of neglect are described in the following sections.

Failure to Thrive

Failure to thrive is defined as the failure to grow or develop at a normal rate during the stages of infancy through early childhood. In some children, this condition is caused by a birth defect; in others, it is the result of a parenting defect. While some parents have no emotional contact with their children, other parents simply do not know how to nurture a child.

Children, like adults, need to feel warmth, affection, and love. Without these elements, some children refuse to grow, gain weight, or develop normally. In more serious cases, failure to thrive results in death.

Fortunately, early detection of this condition can lead to a reversal of the negative development and to miraculous improvement. Treatment usually requires placing the child in a loving, nurturing environment.

Filth and Infestation

Homes that have been reported to child-welfare or public-health officials often contain clogged toilets, animal and human feces on the floor, piles of trash, exposed electrical wiring, no water or electricity, and numerous insects and rodents. It is difficult for most people to imagine the filthy and unsanitary conditions that many children experience in these neglectful homes. These conditions can be found in any neighborhood in America—rich or poor.

Environmental Deprivation

Environmental deprivation occurs in a variety of ways and settings. Some parents who are ashamed of a handicapped child hide the child from the world. Other parents feel pity for a fragile, unhealthy child and overprotect him or her so that the child fails to develop because of lack of stimuli. The children of certain cult members suffer because of their parents' religious beliefs; others suffer nutritional deprivation due to their parents' eating practices. Mentally handicapped parents quite frequently fail to give proper stimulus, care, and direction to their children.

Medical Deprivation

Medical deprivation occurs because many parents simply do not know when and why a child should see a doctor. It also occurs when children are refused medical treatment because of their parents' religious beliefs or because their parents are unable to afford medical care. Some parents who physically injure their children either delay seeking treatment for the children or deny them treatment altogether lest the abuse be detected.

Exposure

Parents who are frustrated by a child's crying sometimes put the child outside in order to gain control again. Some parents lock their children out of the house at dawn and allow them back in the house only when the parents return from work at the end of the day. Some children are left out in the cold to fend for themselves, while others receive second-degree burns from sun exposure. One woman left her three-year-old in the backyard in the rain, without a coat, for several hours because she was so frustrated with the child.

Closeting

Closeting a child may be a parent's way of escaping from the child's crying or a way of punishing a child who has misbehaved. It may also be a parent's way of hiding the shame of a handicapped or retarded child. Closeting may last for a few hours or for years. Attics and basements are convenient and help muffle the child's screams or crying. Some children, in addition to being locked up, are chained and tied in place to prevent their escape.

Sexual Abuse

Sexual abuse, which encompasses a wide variety of inappropriate behaviors, generally involves the sexual mistreatment of a child by an adult or an older child. These behaviors may be direct or indirect in nature.

Indirect sexual abuse includes voyeurism (observing a child undress, bathe, or urinate), an adult or older child exposing his or her genitals to a minor, and pornography (photographing nudity or explicit acts, or showing pornographic materials to a child).

Direct sexual abuse may consist of lingering and intimate kissing, fondling (the adult touching the child's private parts or the adult having the child fondle his or her genitalia), masturbation (either child or adult, with the other observing or both together), oral-genital contact, or digital or penile penetration (vaginal or rectal).

In her book *Betrayal of Innocence*, Susan Forward addresses the various relationships that may be involved in sexual abuse. The chapters discuss sexually abusive relationships between father and daughter, father and son, mother and son, mother and daughter, grandfather and granddaughter, and siblings. Sexual abuse occurring outside the family may involve friends, authority figures, neighbors, or extended family members. Rarely is sexual abuse committed by someone whom the child does not know.

The sexual assault of children is one of the most common forms of child abuse. A nationwide poll conducted by the *Los Angeles Times* concluded that at least twenty-two percent of Americans have been victims of child sexual abuse. Twenty-seven percent of the women and sixteen percent of the men who participated in a random telephone poll said they had been sexually abused as children. According to research by David Finkelhor, approximately one third of our children, male and female, will experience some form of sexual abuse before their eighteenth birthday.

Most perpetrators of sexual abuse are males who are related to the child by blood, marriage, or close association with the mother. Stepfathers have been found to be high on the probability list. While sexual abuse occurs to children of all ages, most incestuous relationships begin when the child is about eight or nine years old and continue through the child's years in junior-high school. In many cases, the abuse begins when the child is very young and continues until the child leaves home.

Generally, once a direct act of sexual abuse has been committed, the abuser fears detection and begins the process of covering up. The person then loads guilt and responsibility onto the child, saying such things as "If you tell, Mom and I will get a divorce and you won't have a father," "If you tell, I won't love you anymore," or "If you tell, the family will break up and it will be all your fault."

An abusive person who is not a family member may also threaten to kill the child and his or her pet or parents, and may use the child's desires as leverage, saying such things as "If you tell, you can't be on the baseball team," or "If you don't tell, I'll let you play." In the case of an older child, the abuser may suggest that he was seduced by the child, shifting shame and responsibility to the victim.

The younger the victim, the more likely the child is to consider the activity to be a show of affection. Most children do not have the sophistication to understand where normal love leaves off and where molestation begins. One adult woman I met told me that throughout her elementary- and high-school years, she slept with her father; her mother had a separate room. She did not realize that this was unusual until she went away to college.

In homes where emotional neglect occurs, some victims of sexual abuse report feeling loved and important only during the sexual acts that were forced upon them. Even though they thought it was wrong, they yearned for the love and affirmation they felt while being molested. When sexual abuse is committed by a person outside the family, the child victim often is lured into acceptance because of the special treats and favors the abuser provides.

Emotional Abuse

One of the most difficult-to-define areas of child abuse is mental or emotional abuse. It is difficult to draw the line between poor parental functioning and the infliction of psychological trauma. Is the parent who continually screams at a child abusing that child? If parents fight in front of their child, is that harmful to the child's positive emotional development?

Emotional abuse also is known as mental abuse, emotional maltreatment, verbal assault, verbal abuse, and psychological abuse. It may be defined as any "chronic and persistent act by an adult that endangers the mental health or emotional development of a child. It is a series of acts, or lack of action that deprives the child of needed love, affection, support and encouragement to grow into a healthy adult" (San Francisco Child Abuse Council).

The old saying "Sticks and stones may break my bones, but words will never hurt me" simply is not true. A continual barrage of negative words may dramatically affect the child's growth and development. A person who repeatedly has been told that he or she is "no good" experiences much emotional pain.

Mental abuse occurs when a child is made to feel worthless, unwanted, and unloved. A child suffers from emotional abuse when someone continually puts him or her down by yelling, calling names, and making him or her feel "no good." Many people believe that the scars of emotional abuse last much longer than those of physical abuse. Emotional abuse leaves the victim with insecurity, low self-esteem, and self-doubt that may linger throughout his or her lifetime.

Emotional or mental abuse may occur in different ways as described in the following sections.

Degradation and Ridicule

Adults who feel controlled by their environment and who are experiencing pressure often strike out verbally at the only person who does not control them or who will not fight back. Examples of verbal abuse include "You're the worst kid I've ever seen," "You idiot; you're really stupid," "Can't you do anything right?," "You'll never amount to anything," and "I wish you'd never been born!" Commonly used terms include stupid, dumb, ignorant, bad, rotten, no good, and ugly. Continual harassment may destroy a child's self-image and will to achieve; cause the child to feel unattractive and stupid; and may even lead him or her to lash out at him or herself, at others, or at society.

Family Violence

A child may also experience psychological trauma when witnessing violence in the home. Unfortunately, spousal abuse (previously referred to as wife beating) is a common phenomenon in today's society. When a child observes parents fighting and inflicting physical harm, he or she often feels afraid and confused. Additionally, some children who witness violence in the home believe that they were the cause of the parents' fighting, a belief that adds feelings of guilt and responsibility. In family violence, there are no winners. These children also experience insecurity as they wonder whether or not the family will break up.

Separation and Divorce

Many divorcing adults, overcome by anger at their spouses, use their children in unhealthy ways. For some, the children are made to be the "go-betweens," conveying messages from parent to parent. Others vent their anger at the ex-spouse in front of the children by revealing negative (and sometimes distorted) information, saying such things as "Your father's no good," "Your mother is a liar," or "I never want you to be like your dad." Often, in custody cases, children are forced to take sides and choose between parents. When this happens, the child becomes a victim and experiences much psychological trauma.

Another situation in which separation and divorce lead to emotional abuse occurs when one parent projects negative feelings about the other parent onto the child. The anger and hostility the parent felt toward the divorced spouse is directed toward the child.

Additional Abuse Situations

There are a number of other types of abuse. They may be equally if not more difficult to recognize. They include the following.

Sibling or Babysitter Abuse

Two areas of child abuse seldom mentioned are sibling and babysitter abuse. Both areas often escape reporting because they are uncommon and often involve abuse by another minor.

Sibling abuse—All brothers and sisters fight among themselves at one time or another. The difference between normal family relationships (in which some fighting occurs) and the relationships in which sibling abuse occurs is the parents' attitude and example. Parents who deal with their anger in physically abusive ways (with each other and/or with the children) and who tolerate excessive physical fighting among the children are not providing the proper example or supervision needed to deter abuse among siblings.

Jealousy and rivalry usually are the causes of sibling abuse when they remain unchecked by the parents. Child abuse is a repetitive process of injury, whether the injury is inflicted by an adult or by another minor. Children and youth can be just as abusive as adults.

Cases of sexual abuse have also been revealed where a sibling or other minor forced a younger child to engage in or perform sexual acts. These young offenders usually have also been victims of sexual abuse.

Babysitter abuse—The public image of a babysitter as the nurturing grandparent or girl next door may be accurate in many cases. Some babysitters, however, are under as much or more stress as abusive parents are and thus become part of the child-abuse problem.

Unfortunately, babysitters often are chosen for reasons such as availability, convenience, proximity, and low cost as opposed to maturity, experience, and trustworthiness. Many lack the knowledge needed to attend to young children properly, especially because many babysitters are young themselves.

Some years ago, for example, *The Los Angeles Times* (September 1976) reported that a three-year-old toddler had been left in the care of a thirteen-year-old babysitter while the mother went to a movie. The babysitter could not get the child to obey, so she called her seventeen-year-old boyfriend. He helped her by beating the child. When the mother returned, the child was dead.

Another incident occurred when a jealous babysitter poured boiling water over the baby under her care after she observed the parents kissing and hugging it goodbye as they left. The child was receiving more love than she was. Earlier that day, her boyfriend had left her for another girl.

Institutional Abuse

A 1988 study of abuse in day-care situations conducted by David Finkelhor, reported that 8.9 children per 10,000 under the age of six were likely to be abused in their own homes. In contrast, 5.5 children per 10,000 enrolled were sexually abused in day-care programs. These figures are based on 1985 national reporting figures. What about other situations in which abuse occurs?

Institutional abuse may occur in foster care, in school, at the child-care center, during a recreational or camping experience, or in the hospital setting. It can be overt physical abuse, extreme corporal punishment, sexual abuse, nutritional deprivation, or neglect. Most institutional abuse is quite subtle and therefore hard to detect. Some institutional practices are not criminal or against the rules; they just dehumanize the individual.

A child left in a playpen for hours without human contact, a teenager receiving lengthy and continual solitary confinement for discipline, and a child not given meals due to misbehavior are possible examples of institutional abuse.

Elder and Dependent Abuse

Although this book focuses on the abuse of minors, it is important for those in the people professions to be aware of the laws that require the reporting of abuse of elder and dependent individuals. Under California law, for example, an elder is an individual sixty-five years of age or older; dependent adults are those between eighteen and sixty-four who have mental or physical limitations that restrict their ability to protect their own rights and to engage in normal activities. Many of these people are cared for by relatives or by residential-care facilities such as nursing homes, convalescent hospitals, mental hospitals, and residential treatment centers.

Reports are to be made when an observed incident or injury appears to reflect abuse and when an individual reports treatment that could be considered abusive.

Reportable conditions include physical or sexual abuse, "unreasonable physical constraint, or prolonged or continual deprivation of food or water," and "use of physical or chemical restraint, medication, or isolation without authorization, or for a purpose other than that for which it was ordered, including, but not limited to, for staff convenience, for punishment, or for a period beyond that for which it was ordered.''

Unintentional Abuse

Not all child abuse is intentional. Unintentional abuse includes such behaviors as shaking, tossing, throwing, and grabbing.

Many frustrated people attempt to gain a child's attention by shaking him or her. These people are shocked when told that the shaking of infants and small children is one of the leading causes of death and retardation in the United States.

Those who work with children need to guard their physical actions and aggressiveness, whether they are done in frustration or in fun. Employees and volunteers must not only be educated about the prevalence and recognition of intentional abuse, but also must be warned about the existence and avoidance of unintentional abuse.

Causes of Abuse

What causes abuse? What factors contribute to an abusive situation? What personality characteristics foster an attitude conducive to abusiveness? What conditions enhance the probability of abuse?

This chapter discusses the background, situational, and personality factors that contribute to abusive situations.

Background Indicators

Background indicators of abuse are factors in the abuser's past that may have contributed to the abusive situation.

Victim of Abuse

Most abusers were themselves abused as children. This characteristic is the most consistent risk factor yet identified. It is frequently said that eighty-five percent to ninety percent of abusers were abused as children. These figures, however, need further substantiation.

One study (Swift, 1978) found that ninety percent of convicted sex offenders had been abused as children. This figure does not mean that ninety percent of those abused became sex offenders, but of those convicted, ninety percent were victims before becoming perpetrators.

Victim of Family Violence

In homes where violence is used to express anger, family members commonly deal violently with frustration in their subsequent relationships. In these families, the children often are scapegoats for pent-up frustrations from personal and relationship conflicts.

The Orange County Social Services Agency in Southern California cited the following as common characteristics of battering parents:

1. They were violently or abusively treated (physically or emotionally) when they were children.
2. They tend to repeat the same behavior with their children.
3. They were deprived in childhood, which generally resulted in feelings of rejection and a lack of love and nurturing.
4. As children, they experienced poor self-worth, degrading comments from parents, and inability to do anything right in the eyes of the parents. They were not given opportunities to express or release their own anger.
5. They tend to perpetuate these same feelings into adulthood and tend to be lonely and relatively friendless.

Victim of Substance Abuse

Research has indicated that substance abuse in the home often results in abusive or neglectful behavior. Parents who are too occupied with their next high or who are unable to function due to their inebriated state sometimes exhibit short tempers, neglect their children, or take advantage of their children and their needs.

Lack of Education and Experience in Child Care

In counseling, I discover that many parents do not understand what children can and can't do at various developmental stages. Most parents are never trained in proper child care. One mother left her baby uncovered in the bright sun because he was exhibiting signs of a cold. As a result, the baby developed both a severe sunburn and pneumonia.

What was considered to be appropriate treatment of children in days gone by or in other cultures has often been found to be ineffective and/or inappropriate by current standards and research findings. Nevertheless, many people continue to practice these harmful behaviors, due either to ignorance or to tradition.

Situational Factors

Situational factors include circumstances that enhance the likelihood of abusive behaviors.

Parental Stress

Ever-increasing stress is experienced by most adults today. Financial, marital, and/or job-related problems add frustrations and tend to overload the parent's ability to cope. Too often, the children suffer from the parent's tension.

Social Isolation

Lack of an extended family, close friends, and neighbors tends to isolate parents from helpful advice and shared child care. A parent who has total responsibility for a child without assistance from other adults simply runs out of energy and resources that might prevent a situation from becoming abusive. Many people do not know about or use available support systems and community services. Once a parent has begun the abuse process, he/she is more likely to withdraw for fear of detection, thus perpetuating the problem. The more isolated one becomes, the harder it is for others to hear a cry for help.

Because of social isolation, more and more children either at risk of or already experiencing abuse are becoming involved in organizations that provide services and programs for minors. This may be a parent's only relief at times from 24 hours, seven days a week of child care. Therefore, you are in a key position to help detect and/or deter abuse.

Lack of Maternal-Infant Bonding

The term "bonding" refers to the feelings of attachment a parent develops for the newborn—when he or she mentally accepts responsibility for the child. Sometimes, for various reasons (medical and emotional), the bonding process is delayed. The longer the delay, the higher the risk that the parent and child will not feel connected. Parents who report little or no bonding or attachment are more likely to abuse their children.

If bonding has been delayed, it is not too late for the parent and child to connect. Remember, initial bonding is good, but lifelong bonding is better.

Targeted Children

In some cases of abuse, only one child was poorly treated, while his or her siblings were not. Often, these children at risk seem to be different from their siblings, requiring more of the parent's time and attention or causing the parent increased frustration. The targeted child may be physically or mentally disabled, may have caused the family additional financial strain, may resemble a resented partner, or may be unwanted.

A sad story was recounted in the *Los Angeles Herald Examiner* in 1978. An eight-year-old girl weighing only twenty-five pounds was found lying in a closet. Although the parents had other children in the home who were reasonably well-cared-for, they kept the girl in the closet all her life. The mother later explained that she had not really wanted that child. Further, she resented the child because the birth required an emergency caesarean section, an operation which left a scar so that the mother was no longer comfortable wearing bikini swimsuits.

In counseling single parents, I have found that it is not uncommon for parents to treat one child differently from the others. In many cases, this is because that particular child reminds the parent of the other, now-hated ex-partner.

Financial Problems

Financial pressures also can increase the likelihood of abuse in families. This does not mean that financial problems lead to abuse, only that this added stress may be the straw that breaks the camel's back, leading to inappropriate parental behavior.

Marital/Relationship Problems

Overwhelming stress due to conflicts in relationships may increase the probability of abusive behavior. Problems may lead one partner to seek sexual gratification elsewhere, even with another family member—with or without the partner's knowledge.

Poor and/or Crowded Housing

Poor housing conditions can increase stress and decrease tolerance levels for parents. Studies have repeatedly demonstrated an increase in the level of violence in densely populated areas. Sufficient space leads to greater tolerance for others; less space leads to negative behavior.

Life Crises

The sudden death of a loved one, a natural disaster, a family transition, and other crises can strip a parent of the emotional strength he or she needs in order to cope with the ups and downs of life. Unwanted changes and events remind us of our inability to control life's direction. This feeling can lead to abusive behavior, demonstrating the adult's belief that his or her life is out of control.

Personality Factors

Personality factors include those that stem from a person's personality rather than from the circumstances or background in which he or she was reared. One's personality may cause one to respond to negative events in healthy or destructive ways.

Unrealistic Expectations

Parents who lack understanding of human growth and development may expect physical and psychological development of which the child is incapable. Areas of greatest expectation and risk are the child's ability to return love; to be toilet-trained; to walk, talk, and eat properly; to do what he or she is told; and to remember information. Punishment results when the child fails to meet the adult's requirements and expectations.

Many children are abused simply because the adult interprets the child's failure to comply as disobedience or rejection of his or her wishes. Using force to achieve compliance to an unrealistic expectation is child abuse. These adults need to lower their expectations and to learn more about children's age-related abilities.

Overpunishment

Deviant behavior is not unusual in children. Unfortunately, parents and other adults often find unique and devastating ways to correct undesirable behavior. Punishment can provide emotional relief for the adult under stress. As pressures mount in the adult, his or her need for emotional relief becomes more severe. Punishment, therefore, becomes more severe and abusive. In these cases, the crime does not fit the punishment. This abuse generally becomes more frequent and severe as the adult develops tolerance for his or her behavior and for the injuries to the child.

Poor Self-Image

Adults who do not like themselves have a hard time liking others, including their children. Parents with feelings of low self-worth often transfer these negative feelings onto their children. Children often look and act like their parents, thus reinforcing the parents' low opinion of themselves.

Depression

A depressed person usually feels little self-worth and may project this feeling onto the child. Even in cases where this transference does not occur, the depressed person generally has little energy for others and is self-absorbed. These feelings can result in abusive or neglectful behavior.

Rejection and Role Reversal

An adult who was unloved as a child generally continues to look for that love as a parent. The greater the parent's need for love, the more likely he/she is to depend on a child for that love. Some adults feel rejected by a child who does not show affection in ways that the adult desires. The child does not understand the adult's wishes or is incapable of exhibiting affection in the expected ways.

Some women report having a baby in order to have someone who will love them. The infant who is expected to provide love usually provides wet diapers, cries all night, and adds both financial and emotional strain. These feelings of rejection on the part of the adult breed hostility toward the child. Children need love and are not in a position to give it in the quantities demanded by an unfulfilled adult. Thus, they fail to live up to the adult's needs and often are abused.

Indicators of Abuse

*M*ost victims of abuse do not share their secret with others because of their feelings of guilt, fear, or shame. For this reason, those in occupations working with minors must be aware of the possible behavioral and physical indications of abuse in order to report their suspicions.

Although few of the indicators are conclusive in themselves, when they are considered in conjunction with others, the caregiver can make reports to the local child-abuse authorities with a certain degree of confidence. For example, when counseling a young child who has much more knowledge of sex and sexual behavior than is age-appropriate, consider whether sexual abuse has occurred or is occurring. Watch closely for other possible indications, and strongly consider filing a report with the child-abuse authorities.

Abusive situations often are difficult to detect, because behavioral and observational clues generally are neither obvious nor definitive. It is, therefore, important for those working with children and adolescents to remember and to be conversant in the spectrum of possible indicators and manifestations of abuse when reporting.

For example, bed-wetting is cited as being a possible physical indicator of emotional or physical abuse. If a child at camp is wetting his or her bed, this does not mean that the child *is* being abused at home (or at all for that matter). Many children wet their beds. What it does mean is that this indicator, along with others, should be noted by the staff members. If additional indicators are observed, the employee must be aware of the potential need to make a report of child abuse to the authorities.

Always remember that most indicators should be taken in conjunction with others. Take care not to draw conclusions from any single indicator.

This chapter includes information on the possible indicators of the different types of abuse, listed according to their behavioral and physical manifestations. Information on wound identification also is provided. A listing of the effects of abuse on people at different developmental stages is presented in Appendix P.

Indicators of Sexual Abuse

Behavioral Indicators

1. Is reluctant to change clothes in front of others.
2. Is withdrawn.
3. Exhibits sexualized behavior: unusual sexual behavior and/or knowledge beyond that which is common for his or her particular developmental stage.
4. Has poor peer relationships.
5. Either avoids or seeks out adults.
6. Is pseudomature.
7. Is manipulative.
8. Is self-conscious.
9. Has problems with authority and rules.
10. Exhibits an eating disorder.
11. Is self-mutilating.
12. Is obsessively clean.
13. Uses or abuses alcohol and/or other drugs.
14. Exhibits delinquent behavior, such as running away from home.

15. Exhibits extreme compliance or defiance.
16. Is fearful or anxious.
17. Exhibits suicidal gestures and/or attempts suicide.
18. Is promiscuous.
19. Engages in fantasy or infantile behavior.
20. Is unwilling to participate in sports activities.
21. Has school difficulties.

Physical Indicators

1. Has pain and/or itching in the genital area.
2. Has bruises or bleeding in the genital area.
3. Has venereal disease.
4. Has swollen private parts.
5. Has difficulty walking or sitting.
6. Has torn, bloody, and/or stained underclothing.
7. Experiences pain when urinating.
8. Is pregnant.
9. Has vaginal or penile discharge.
10. Wets the bed.

Indicators of Neglect

Behavioral Indicators

1. Is truant or tardy to school often or arrives early and stays late.
2. Begs or steals food.
3. Attempts suicide.
4. Uses or abuses alcohol and/or other drugs.
5. Is extremely dependent or detached.
6. Engages in delinquent behavior, such as prostitution or stealing.
7. Appears to be exhausted.
8. States frequent or continual absence of parent or guardian.

Physical Indicators

1. Frequently is dirty, unwashed, hungry, or inappropriately dressed.
2. Engages in dangerous activities (possibly because he or she generally is unsupervised).
3. Is tired and listless.
4. Has unattended physical problems.
5. May appear to be overworked and/or exploited.

Indicators of Emotional Abuse

Behavioral Indicators

1. Is overly eager to please.
2. Seeks adult contact.
3. Views abuse as being warranted.
4. Exhibits changes in behavior.
5. Is excessively anxious.
6. Is depressed.
7. Is unwilling to discuss problems.
8. Exhibits aggressive or bizarre behavior.
9. Is withdrawn.
10. Is apathetic.
11. Is passive.
12. Has unprovoked fits of yelling or screaming.
13. Exhibits inconsistent behavior at home and school.
14. Feels responsible for the abuser.
15. Runs away from home.
16. Attempts suicide.
17. Has low self-esteem.
18. Exhibits a gradual impairment of health and/or personality.
19. Has difficulty sustaining relationships.
20. Has unrealistic goals.
21. Is impatient.

22. Is unable to communicate or express his or her feelings, needs, or desires.
23. Sabotages his or her chances of success.
24. Lacks self-confidence.
25. Is self-deprecating and has a negative self-image.

Physical Indicators

1. Has a sleep disorder, including nightmares or restlessness.
2. Wets the bed.
3. Exhibits developmental lags (stunting of his or her physical, emotional, and/or mental growth).
4. Is hyperactive.
5. Exhibits an eating disorder.

Indicators of Physical Abuse

Behavioral Indicators

1. Is wary of adults.
2. Is either extremely aggressive or withdrawn.
3. Is dependent and indiscriminate in his or her attachments.
4. Is uncomfortable when other children cry.
5. Generally controls his or her own crying.
6. Exhibits a drastic behavior change when not with parents or caregiver.
7. Is manipulative.
8. Has a poor self-concept.
9. Exhibits delinquent behavior, such as running away from home.
10. Uses or abuses alcohol and/or other drugs.
11. Is self-mutilating.
12. Is frightened of parents or of going home.
13. Is overprotective of or responsible for parents.

14. Exhibits suicidal gestures and/or attempts suicide.
15. Has behavior problems at school.

Physical Indicators

1. Has unexplained* bruises or welts, often clustered or in a pattern.
2. Has unexplained* and/or unusual burns (cigarette, doughnut-shaped, immersion-line, object-patterned).
3. Has unexplained* bite marks.
4. Has unexplained* fractures or dislocations.
5. Has unexplained* abrasions or lacerations.
6. Wets the bed.

(* Or explanation is inconsistent or improbable.)

Physical Abuse Described—Wound Identification

Shin or knee scrapes on children are both normal and expected. Children who run and play frequently trip, fall, and bump into things. These injuries usually follow a pattern prescribed by age and activity. The bony prominences that children most frequently scrape or bruise in play activity or in accidents are the knees, elbows, forehead, hands, chin, and nose. If a child's injuries don't match the pattern for his or her age, child abuse should be considered.

Fundamental comparison of the explanation with the actual injuries usually either confirms an accident or shows a difference between the explanation and the actual injuries. Parents or care providers who abuse children make up explanations to avoid detection. Frequently, they invent these explanations on the spur of the moment or under pressure of questioning.

Primary Target Zone

The primary target zone for physical abuse extends from the back of the neck to the backs of the knees, including the backs of the arms and hands—areas that may be injured when the child tries to defend him or herself. Injuries in the primary target zone are considered suspicious due to the fact that seventy percent of nonaccidental injuries occur in this area of the body. Figure 5.1 indicates this area. (See page 46.)

The following sections describe the most common forms of physical abuse. The type and pattern of injuries can be significant in early detection.

Although the following written information can be helpful, visual training is a better way to learn to recognize physical abuse. For Kids Sake, Inc., offers a thorough slide presentation that portrays various injuries caused by abuse.

Bruises and Welts

Separate studies done by D.G. Gil (1971) and James Mead (1977) indicate that bruises and welts are the most common injuries suffered by abused children. Gil and Mead reported that approximately seventy percent of physical abuse of children involves these types of injuries.

Multiple Injuries

Approximately thirty-two percent of reported incidents of physical abuse involve multiple injuries. Multiple injuries consist of abrasions, contusions, and lacerations. Other indicators are welts and scar-tissue injuries in multiple stages of healing, such as burns, scratches, lacerations and bruises of various colors.

In a probable child-abuse case, it is important to look for a series of injuries. Mead's study found that when an adult loses control and strikes a child, he or she very rarely strikes the child only once.

Wraparound Injuries

Another warning sign of physical abuse is the wraparound injury. This kind of injury is caused by a flexible object, such as a strap, belt, or cord. An extension cord leaves marks of a consistent

Figure 5.1 *Primary Target Zone*

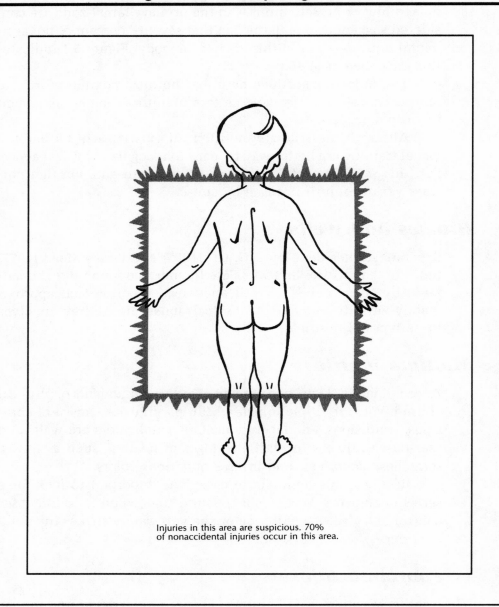

Injuries in this area are suspicious. 70%
of nonaccidental injuries occur in this area.

thickness, whereas belt wounds leave both thin and wide marks in a looping fashion due to the centrifugal force that turns the belt.

Some angry parents and caretakers constrain children by tying them up. They may tie them to a bed or place them in a closet or another room for a long period. Abrasions to the neck, ankles, and wrists generally result as the constraining material (rope, belt, cord, or whatever) rubs against the child's skin.

Imprint of an Object on the Skin

Often, injuries indicate what object was used. Injuries from belt buckles, hose couplings, hands, fists, rings, or spoons leave marks that provide unequivocal evidence of trauma to soft tissue. The tongue of a belt makes a whipping action that creates a hook-shaped cut shaped like a gull's wing. These wounds most often appear in clusters.

Another type of injury that is not always noticeable, occurs when a caretaker uses a spoon to hit a child on the head. Wounds caused by the "spoon trick" can be detected only by feeling the child's scalp for multiple lumps.

Fixed-Object Lacerations

This type of laceration results from a stick, switch, coat hanger, ruler, or any other fixed object. Lacerations of this type usually appear on the upper part of the legs, buttocks, or lower back. The resulting pattern is referred to as "series straight-line lacerations."

Pummeling

Pummeling refers to blows from a heavy blunt object, such as a baseball bat or an adult's fist, on soft tissue and results in deep muscular hemorrhage. Such injuries are readily palpable and rarely discolor. In time, the collection of blood calcifies and is visible on X rays.

Fractures (Excluding Skull)

Children complaining of pain from possible broken bones should receive immediate medical attention. All suspected cases of child abuse should include a series of long-bone X rays. Long-bone fractures that are torsion-induced are characterized as spiral fractures of the mid-shaft or as evulsion fractures of the ankle, knee, wrist, or elbow joints. These may be the result of an adult swinging a child by an extremity. According to Mead's study, the chances that a spiral fracture will occur any other way are very slight. X rays also are needed to detect any previous untreated fractures.

Skull and Head Injuries

Any injury to the skull or head, no matter how slight it may seem to be, should receive immediate medical attention. Head injuries are the most common cause of death as a result of physical abuse. Skull X rays may reveal an eggshell fracture of the back of the skull. Because accidental injury to the head usually involves the shoulders, a blow to the skull rarely produces more than a single crack. When a child is slammed or thrown against a wall, however, the back of his or her head shatters in a multi-radiant fashion.

Blows to the head also frequently cause subdural hemorrhage and subdural hematoma, which is a bruiselike brain injury that can create pressure resulting in mental retardation, paralysis, or death. Subdural hematoma does not always result immediately. The child may appear to be acting normally, but pressure could be building up in the child's head and the child could die within twenty-four hours.

Beating or striking a child in the head may cause serious injuries without causing the types of abrasions that would result from an accident or a fall. If a child falls accidentally, he or she probably will injure only one surface plane of the head. Except in auto accidents, injuries to both sides of the head are very uncommon, so multiple-plane injuries are indications of probable abuse.

Geographic Burns and Scalding

Geographic burns are characteristic of the shape of the hot object evenly burned into a child's skin, e.g. the grill of an electric heater, or the burner element of an electric stove. An electric stove's burner element leaves a coil-shaped burn, whereas a gas stove's burner element leaves a star-shaped or circular pattern.

When a child is held by the hands and legs under a faucet from which hot water is running, the tissue on his or her abdomen and upper legs folds up, preventing burning in the creases. Injuries of this type are referred to as *zebra burns*.

As a child steps into a tub of hot water, the reflex response is to sit down, resulting in burns to the feet and the entire surface of the buttocks. When a child has been forcibly held in a sitting position in hot water, however, the center area of the buttocks, if pressed tightly against the tub, is spared from burning. This results in a doughnut-shaped burn on the buttocks or slightly above.

Immersion burns to the extremities also are common among child-abuse victims. One example that does not appear to be accidental is a scald burn between the shoulder blades—the result of immersion of a child's upper back in hot water. Toddlers who are not toilet-trained often receive dipping-type burns to the buttocks. This type of burn, appearing as an oval around the genital area, occurs when an adult dips the child into scalding water out of frustration (often over the smell or mess of the child's wet or soiled diaper).

Older children may experience *glove burns* (burns to the hands) or *stocking burns* (burns to the feet and ankles) as a parent or adult's misguided, abusive form of discipline to teach a child a lesson for touching something or going somewhere that he or she shouldn't have.

In burn situations, it is very simple to differentiate between accidental or inflicted (child abuse) injuries. The type and severity of the burn usually give a clue as to how it happened. For example, if a child received a burn on the fingers from a pot of boiling water, it would be slight if accidental because the natural instinct would be to immediately remove the fingers. A more serious burn, resulting from longer exposure to the water, would be present if an adult had held the child's fingers in the water.

Cigarette burns are identified by deep, round burns that are a little larger than the end of the cigarette. They are frequently found on the backs of the hands, on the feet, on the large areas of the chest, and even on the face.

Wound Identification Summary

Bruises—What to Look for

1. Bruises that are different colors (in various stages of healing).
2. Bruises to the back, buttocks, and backs of legs.
3. Bruises in groups or patterns.
4. Bruises that are not common for the age and activity level of the child.
5. Defense wounds to the backs of the arms and hands.

Lacerations—What to Look for

1. Loop type lacerations from belts, straps, and extension cords.
2. Lacerations to the back side of the body.
3. Series or groups of straight-line lacerations or welts.
4. Overlapping injuries on top of previous injuries.
5. Scars from previous injuries.

Head Injuries—What to Look for

1. Black eyes.
2. Split lips.
3. Any series of lumps.
4. Loose or missing teeth.
5. Eggshell skull fractures.
6. Facial bruises.
7. Jaw and nose fractures.

Fractures and Skeletal Injuries—What to Look for

1. Spiral fractures (injuries caused by twisting or pulling).
2. Rib fractures.

Burns—What to Look for

1. Immersion lines.
2. Demarcation lines or outlines.
3. Burns to the buttocks or genitals.
4. Cigarette burns.
5. Burns to the hands (punishment for playing with matches).
6. Rope burns that indicate confinement.

Reporting Requirements

*T*hose who work with young people likely will come across a child or teen who is suspected to have been abused or who states that he or she is being abused. According to the various state laws on child abuse, when this happens, you must report the suspected abuse.

The reporting laws basically state that anyone whose employment or volunteer position involves contact with minors is a *mandated reporter*. Anyone *may* report, but those who work with children *must* report. In some states, even those in commercial film and photography businesses are mandated reporters in the event that they find evidence of pornographic material involving minors. Reporting laws vary somewhat from state to state (and province to province in Canada), but they all stress the importance of notifying the appropriate authorities.

Reporting Facts and Responsibilities

Every state maintains a mandatory child-abuse reporting law. Although there are some differences in states' requirements, these laws generally cover most of the information listed in the following sections.

Who the Mandated Reporters Are

Those who, by the nature of their employment, have contact with children are mandated reporters. These people include the following:

Medical workers: physicians, surgeons, nurses, dentists, residents, interns, pediatricians, chiropractors, psychologists, psychiatrists.

Public/private workers: employees of public and private schools, child-care personnel, resident and day-camp employees, social workers, peace and probation officers, members of the clergy and other youth ministry practitioners, child-welfare supervisors, certified public personnel.

Commercial film or photographic print processors (in specified instances, in some states).

Anyone with reasonable grounds to believe a child is in need of protection. Some states and provinces require anyone to report when he or she has reasonable grounds to believe that a child has been or is likely to be abused.

What Must Be Reported

Abuse, neglect, and/or abandonment.
Deliberate physical injury of a child.
Sexual molestation.
Causing or allowing a child great bodily harm, death,
    unjustifiable physical pain or mental suffering, or
    danger to health.
Exploitation, child pornography, and child prostitution.

When to Report

Report any observations, knowledge, or reasonable suspicion of abuse immediately by telephone and in writing. Some states/provinces specify within twenty-four to thirty-six hours.

Where to Report

Depending on your state or province, report the suspected abuse to one of the following authorities:

Police department.
Probation department.
Welfare department or health department.
Department of social services.
Children's protective services.
Also check the Yellow Pages under "child abuse."

Note: If the child resides in a different area from the one where the discovery of abuse was made, some states prefer that reports be made to your local authorities, while others prefer that reports be filed with authorities where the minor resides. Still others prefer that reports be filed with the authorities where the alleged abuse occurred. Contact your local authorities for clarification, and keep the information on file.

What to Include in the Report

Name of minor(s),
Address of minor(s),
Extent and nature of injury or molestation.

Refer to chapter seven for more information on what to report.

Acknowledging Reporting Requirements

In some states there is an additional requirement for those who are mandated reporters. Each employer, employee, and volunteer must sign a form acknowledging his or her awareness of the reporting requirements and the accompanying responsibilities. This form should include a summary of state law and the procedures that the mandated reporter must follow.

A sample mandated reporter acknowledgment form is included in Appendix A.

Reporting Concerns and Questions

Once you are involved in a situation that requires a report be made, even when you understand your responsibilities as a reporter, there may be a number of concerns and questions that seem unanswered. The answers to some of these questions are in the following sections.

Should I Report?—Lack of Solid Evidence

As a mandated reporter, you are to report any *known* or *suspected* child abuse or neglect. The word "suspected" is used to emphasize the fact that you need not be the one who decides whether the abuse actually occurred; your job is to report what you have heard or observed. You must report even when you are unsure whether the abuse occurred or is occurring.

If you do not report, you could indirectly be assisting a child abuser. Most offenders abuse or molest more than one child. By not reporting, you may unknowingly and unwillingly be enabling the alleged criminal to damage other children.

Most states require that reports be made when there is "reasonable suspicion." Based on your knowledge of the possible indicators of abuse and the basics of wound identification (presented in chapter five), you should be able to make such reports.

Even though your report may not be based on solid evidence or known facts, it can assist in the detection of abuse. In order to help identify abuse, many states have established a central index that enables cross-checking of reports. If several other reports that lacked substantial evidence had been filed naming the same alleged abuser, the investigating authorities would have sufficient information on which to proceed. Therefore, it is imperative that you always make reports of child abuse, even when the information seems insignificant.

One youth worker with whom I spoke informed me that he would make reports only if he saw the abuse himself or had solid evidence that it had occurred. I cautioned him that in the majority of cases, the abuse is well-hidden from sight and suspicion. Sometimes, the smallest clue can be the key to exposing an unhealthy or traumatic situation.

I was told by a licensed clinical social worker from a children's protective-service office that he often receives reports that do not appear to be substantial but that upon investigation, prove to be serious and well-founded. In almost every case, the reporter questioned whether he or she should have informed the authorities, due to the fact that the report was based on little solid evidence.

It also is important, as is discussed in chapter nine, that you report any revealed abuse. Some mandated reporters are hesitant to believe the young person, especially if they have reason to question his or her character or behavior. As stated, you must report any known, revealed, or suspected abuse.

When a child tells you about an abusive situation, you need not personally determine whether the child is telling the truth or is lying; that is the job of the children's welfare officer. Simply share the revealed information with the authorities, and let them determine what course of action is necessary. Remember, you will not be held liable for an unfounded report (unless it can be determined that you acted maliciously), but you could be held accountable for *not* making a report. Many in the field of child-abuse prevention believe that it is better to err in the direction of overreporting than underreporting. I agree.

What Could Happen If I Don't Report?— Liability

Legally mandated reporters can be held criminally liable if they fail to report knowledge or suspicion of abuse. For instance, under California law, if you are aware of or suspect abuse and do not report it, you can be charged with a misdemeanor (with a fine of up to one thousand dollars and six months in jail), and a civil suit can be filed against you for any later damage incurred on the victim. The law clearly emphasizes the importance of reporting.

What Happens When a Report Is Made?

When a report is submitted, it usually is placed in one of three categories.

First, if the report contains substantial evidence, the authorities usually visit the child. The representative will attempt to verify what happened, who the alleged abuser was, and where the abuse occurred. If abuse is determined to be highly likely, the agency takes immediate action to ensure the safety of the victim.

Second, the report may be placed on file (and in a statewide central index) due to a lack of evidence. In these instances, as already mentioned, if another report is made naming the same alleged perpetrator, the authorities have more cause to pursue an investigation.

In the third category, the case is dropped because, upon investigation, the report is determined to be unfounded.

Could There Be Repercussions?—Immunity

Legally mandated reporters have immunity when making a report. No reporter can legally be dismissed, disciplined, or harassed for filing a report of suspected child abuse. If the alleged abuser decides to sue the reporter for damages, most states provide immunity and funding to cover any legal fees. The courts will act against a reporter only if it is determined that he or she made the report for malicious reasons, rather than because he or she had actual suspicion or knowledge of child abuse.

In some cases of child abuse, the alleged abuser accuses the child's mother of filing a false report. When the alleged abuser is the child's father or stepfather, he often claims that the mother was angry about a divorce or breakup. These "malicious moms" or "dirty divorce" cases, as they often are called, generally contain well-founded reports. Many of the mothers, who were afraid to report previously, for economic or emotional reasons, finally felt free to reveal their knowledge or suspicion of abuse.

Will the Alleged Abuser Know Who Made the Report?—Confidentiality

Mandated reporters must give their names when they make a report, whereas nonmandated reporters may report anonymously. In most states, however, the mandated reporter's name will be kept confidential unless a court orders the information to be disclosed.

The alleged abuser is not given the reporter's name unless you chose to inform him or her yourself or unless the case goes to trial and you are accused of filing a malicious false report.

The timing of an investigation or an innocent remark may inadvertently reveal the source of a previously anonymous child-abuse report. This can result in the child's being barred by the parent from returning to the youth program, friend's homes, or school. It is important to remember, however, that concern about losing the child's participation in a potentially valuable program should *not* make you hesitate to report.

What If My Supervisor Refuses to File a Report?

If you share suspicion or knowledge of abuse with your supervisor, who refuses to make a report, you must make a report yourself. If the supervisor does file a report, you need not file also; only one report is necessary.

Will the Abuser Be Arrested?

Depending on the evidence, the laws of your state or province, and what actually happened, the abuser or molester may or may not be arrested. The decision to arrest usually is made by the district or governmental attorney, based on the information and evidence collected by the investigating agency.

Will the Child Be Interviewed Repeatedly?

The child should not be interviewed repeatedly. The nonabusing parent or guardian should insist that someone who is well-trained in interviewing abused children conduct the session and that the session be videotaped, if possible, for viewing by others who need the information.

Will the Child Have to Testify?

Fewer than ten percent of all abuse cases actually go to trial. If the child must testify, he or she should visit the courtroom, the judge, and the district or government-appointed attorney ahead of time. In some cases, videotapes have been used in place of personal courtroom testimony by the victim.

If you are in a position where you have ongoing contact with a child who reveals an abuse, for example in an after school program, you may have the opportunity to assist in helping to prepare the child for court. If you are in a position where an abused child is in your care for only a short period, for example a one week session of resident camp, you may never have the opportunity to assist with familiarizing the child with the court room.

Reporting Laws

Reporting laws vary somewhat from state to state and province to province but have many similarities. Each employee or volunteer who has contact with minors must be aware of the specific requirements and responsibilities outlined in the state in which he or she works.

In Arizona, for example, mandated reporters include "any physician, hospital intern, dentist, osteopath, chiropractor, podiatrist, country medical examiner, nurse, psychologist, school personnel, social worker, peace officer, parent or counselor, or any other person having responsibility for the care or treatment of children." In British Columbia, Florida, Indiana, New Hampshire, New Jersey, New Mexico, North Carolina, Rhode Island, and Wyoming—the law simply says that a mandated reporter is *any person* who knows or has reason to suspect that a child has been abused or neglected.

Reportable conditions include those in which the mandated reporter "has reason to suspect that a child has been injured as a result of physical, mental or emotional abuse, or neglect or sexual abuse" (Kansas), "has reason to believe that a child . . . has suffered any wound, injury, disability, or other condition of such nature as to reasonably indicate abuse or neglect" (Ohio), or has "reason/cause to believe that a child's physical or mental health or welfare has been or may be adversely affected by abuse or neglect" (South Carolina and Texas), or has "reasonable grounds to believe that a child is in need of protection" (British Columbia).

Penalties for nonreporting may include a fine of "not more than five hundred dollars" (Alabama, Colorado, Connecticut, Louisiana, Maine, South Carolina, and Vermont) or "not more than one thousand dollars" (California, Massachusetts, Oregon, and Wisconsin). In most states, nonreporting is a misdemeanor, but many states add that the nonreporter may be assessed civil liability for damages resulting from failure to report. In New York, for example, the penalties for nonreporting are "a Class A misdemeanor; civil liability for damages resulting from failure to report."

Appendices B and C include an example of a state reporting law (Massachusetts) and of a child abuse report form (California).

For specific information about laws, agencies, and procedures for reporting child abuse call the National Child Abuse Hotline at 1-800-4-A-CHILD. In Canada, call the National Clearinghouse on Family Violence at 1-800-267-1291.

For more information on organizations and support groups, see Appendix E.

PART II

Working with Abuse Victims

▶ Those who work with young people generally encounter child abuse in one of four ways. They suspect that a program participant is being abused; they are told by a child that he or she is being abused; they themselves or a fellow staff member was abused as a child; or they themselves or fellow staff members have been accused of child abuse.

▶ Part II provides information on how to deal with the first three of these four situations. This section will explain what to do, how to report, and how to work with a person who has been abused. Accusations of abuse are addressed in both Part II and Part III.

What to Do When You Suspect or Discover Child Abuse

On the last night of camp, after the closing campfire, Susie asked to talk with her counselor . . . alone. The look on her face told the counselor that it was important.

After returning to the cabin and making sure everyone was reasonably well-behaved, the counselor took Susie outside on the porch to talk. Susie seemed uncomfortable, not with the staff member but with what she wanted to share. The counselor sensed her uneasiness and reminded Susie of the care and concern she had for the child. Then Susie began to tell her story.

Susie told the counselor she was being sexually abused by an uncle. "I've never told anyone before. I was ashamed and scared," she said. Tears streamed down her face as she recounted the horrors of the numerous encounters. "I've wanted to tell someone for so long, but didn't know who I could trust or who would understand . . . until now."

Youth Service Organizations Are Often the First to Know

Susie's situation is not uncommon. Due to the nature of their work, staff members of organizations that provide programs and services for minors often are the first to discover or suspect child abuse or neglect. These child-care providers generally have ongoing contact with children and adolescents. This daily or weekly interaction often enables youth workers to observe the effects of abuse or to hear about it directly from children.

Therefore, those who have this contact with children are in a unique position to learn about abusive situations, due to the close nature of the relationships they develop. Many children form special friendships with a staff member, teacher, counselor, or recreation leader. In this close relationship, the child feels comfortable and safe and may risk telling his or her secret or sharing his or her fear. You may be the first to hear about abuse.

Similarly, daily or weekly involvement with children often enables youth workers to be the first to observe the indicators of abuse mentioned in chapter five. Whether or not the young person discusses abuse, youth workers have a unique opportunity to observe the possible symptoms of abuse.

If Susie had confided her secret to you, what would you have done?

One camp director said he would make a report only after interviewing the camper. He did this in order to determine the worth of the allegation. He did not want to be crying wolf by making unfounded reports to the local authorities. He did not understand the severity and depth of trauma associated with most abusive situations or his need to have only reasonable suspicion.

Many children feel threatened and uncomfortable when they are questioned by an authority figure, because they fear that they have done something wrong. Often, children deny previously told stories of abuse or lie about any injuries they have suffered for fear of getting into trouble. Therefore, it is best not to interrogate or interview the child about the reliability of his or her claim.

Child-protective-service departments are staffed by trained individuals whose primary concern is the welfare of children. They take great care when speaking with an abuse victim to gain the most accurate picture of the alleged incident of abuse. These trained professionals are familiar with appropriate interviewing techniques and seek to minimize the negative impact of questioning on a child. Questions are carefully selected and sensitively posed to avoid implying that certain responses are desirable. The resources and referrals available to them surpass those available to most child-care providers.

Ideally, you will sense both the need for and the importance of reporting possible abuse situations. Remember, you need only *suspect* abuse; you are not the judge and jury. Government officials are the ones who investigate whether abuse has occurred or is occurring.

What to Do and What to Report

I often receive calls from people who work with young people asking what they should do to prepare themselves for disclosures of abuse and how to make reports. These professionals know that they are to report the situation but don't know how to go about it or what they should do or know ahead of time. I suggest that they take the following steps.

Assure Privacy But Not Confidentiality

If possible, whenever a child asks to speak with a staff member and the matter appears to be important (or the child indicates that it is), meet with the child in a place that has few distractions and that is out of earshot but within the view of others.

Often, you will not have the opportunity to plan for such an occasion. But if the counselor who spoke with Susie in the example had not retreated to a quiet location, the child might not have chosen to open up after all. It is important to talk in an environment that seems safe to the child.

In some instances, a child may say, "There is a secret I want to share with you, but only if you promise not to tell anyone else." As a mandated reporter, you cannot make such a promise. What you might choose to say is "Everything that we talk about will be between you and me. It will be confidential unless I think you are going to hurt yourself or someone else, or if someone is hurting you."

Be Calm

If your response to hearing about an abusive situation reflects shock, you may adversely affect the child. It is appropriate to share your feelings of concern with the child, but getting upset about the assault may result in the child's feeling worse about the situation and his or her role in it.

Believe the Child

Do not ask the child "why" questions such as "Why didn't you tell someone sooner?" or "Why did you let it continue?" It is unusual for children to make up stories about sexual or physical abuse. Children who find that adults are unwilling to listen to or believe them generally withdraw and keep an abusive situation a secret. Many children think that adults will not believe them, especially if their abuser has reinforced such thinking by saying, "No one will believe you because you're just a kid," or "Children tell lies and aren't to be believed." Therefore, it is important not to discount anything a child tells you that involves abuse.

Get the Facts—But Don't Interrogate

Before you make a report, you must have certain information. As already mentioned, it is not necessary to interview the child to determine whether the abuse actually occurred; that is the responsibility of trained professionals. Your responsibility is to present certain facts to the authorities.

Although the amount and type of information included on the child-abuse report form varies from state to state and province to province, the information required generally includes the following:

1. Name of the child.
2. Address of the child.
3. Extent of injury or molestation.
4. Your name, address, telephone number, profession, and relationship to the child. (In most states, nonmandated reporters may request anonymity.)

5. The name, address, and telephone number, if known, of the alleged abuser.

It is beneficial, however, to have the following additional information, if possible:

1. The name, address, present whereabouts, gender, and date of birth or estimated age of the child and of any other children in the household.
2. The names, addresses, and telephone numbers of the child's parents or other people responsible for his or her care.
3. The nature and extent of the child's injuries, abuse, or neglect.
4. Any indication of previous injuries, abuse, or neglect.
5. The circumstances under which you first became aware of the child's alleged injuries, abuse, or neglect.
6. If the information was given to you by a third party, the identity of that person, unless he or she requests anonymity.
7. Detail of the incident, as reported by the victim.
8. The primary language spoken by the child and his or her caretaker(s).
9. An assessment of the risk of further harm to the child and, if a risk exists, whether it is imminent.

Massachusetts Department of Social Services.

A sample child-abuse report form and instructions are included in Appendix C. Request copies of your state's form from your state's authorities. Keep this form on file. Have them available.

Reassure the Child

It probably took a lot of courage for the child to finally tell his or her story. Assure the child that what happened was not his or her fault. Use such statements as, "I believe you," "This happens to other kids, too," and "It's not your fault this happened." Encourage the child by telling him or her that he or she did well to tell you.

Get Help When You Have Questions

If you have questions or are uncertain about something, the local agency responsible for child-abuse reports should be willing and able to answer any questions you may have.

If the child resides in a different city, county, or state (as may be the case for many camps and some child-care and recreation programs), you should know where to report possible abuse. Remember, if the child resides in a different area from where your program operates, some states prefer that reports be made to your local authorities; others prefer that reports be filed with the authorities in the area where the child lives. Still others prefer that reports be filed with the authorities in the area where the alleged abuse occurred. Be prepared!

Be Careful About What You Say

It is important to understand the limits of the child-welfare system in your area and to not make promises that may contradict those made by the authorities. Tell the child that it might be tough going; it may not be easy.

The following poem, written by an unknown author, expresses the feelings of many victims.

I asked you for help
and you told me you would.
I told you the things my dad did to me.
It was really hard for me to say all those things
but you told me to trust you
and then you made me repeat them to 14 different
strangers.
I asked you for privacy
and you sent two policemen
to my school in front of everyone
to quote, "go downtown"
for a talk in their black and white car
like I was the one being busted.

I asked you to believe me
and you said you did.
Then you connected me to a lie detector,
took me to court
where lawyers put me on trial
like I was a liar.
I can't help it if I can't remember times or dates
your questions got me confused.
My confusion got you suspicious.

I asked you for help
and you gave me a doctor with a cold metal gadget
and cold hands.
Spread my legs and stared just like my father.
You said it wouldn't hurt
just like my father.
You told me not to cry.
You said I looked fine,
Good news for me you said,
Bad news for my case.

I asked you for confidentiality
and you let the newspaper get my story.
What does it matter that they left out my name,
they put my father's
and our home address.
Even my best friend's mother
won't let her talk to me anymore.

I asked you for protection
and you gave me a social worker
who patted my head
and called me honey.
Mostly because she could never remember my name.
You sent me to live with strangers in another place
and a different school.
I lost my part in a school play
and the science fair,
while he and all the others got to stay home.

(continued)

Do you know what it's like
to live where there's a lock on a refrigerator?
Where you have to ask permission to use the shampoo
or get used to hearing, "Hi, I'm your new social worker;
this is your new foster sister,
dorm mother,
group home."
You tiptoe around like a perpetual guest.
You don't even get to see your own puppy grow up.
    Do you know what it's like to know
more social workers than friends?
    Do you know what it feels like
to be the one that everybody blames
for all the trouble?
Even when they were speaking to me,
all they talked about was lawyers, shrinks, fees,
whether or not they'd lose the mortgage.
    Do you know what it's like when your sisters hate
you and your brother calls you a liar?
My word against my own father's.
I'm twelve years old,
he's the manager of a bank.
You say you believe me,
who cares
nobody else does.
    I asked you for help
and you forced my mom to choose between us,
she chose him of course.
She was scared
and had a lot to lose.
I've had a lot to lose too,
the difference was you never told me how much.
    I asked you to put an end to the abuse
you put an end to my whole family.
You took away my nights of hell

and gave me days of hell instead.
You exchanged my private nightmare for a public one.

Reporting—Again

If, after you have made a report to the local child-abuse agency, you learn about continued or further abuse, make another report. Often, these additional reports enable the authorities to act if the initial reports proved to be inconclusive. Therefore, do not hesitate to report each new incident of suspected abuse, even if you have already filed a report.

Abuse Accusations— Truth or Consequences

A five-year-old boy in your day-care program has strange bruises on his arm. From your studies on child abuse, you feel that the marks look suspicious, and you decide to ask the boy what happened. He seems unusually withdrawn as he tells you that he fell while playing in his house. What would you believe? What would you do?

A teenager in your program discloses that she is being sexually abused by her stepfather. You know the stepfather and have always viewed him as being an outstanding person and community member. The teenager, on the other hand, is an emotional roller coaster, up one minute and down the next—very unpredictable, moody and often with a flair for the dramatic. What would you believe? What would you do?

A girl tells about an adult neighbor who has been making her play "King and Queen" with him. He gives her candy and presents and plays secret games with her. You know this child to have an active imagination, often telling stories about having lived in castles with kings and queens. What would you believe? Whom would you believe? What would you do?

A hyperactive boy reveals that his father has physically abused him. School reports indicate that he has behavioral problems. The father denies the accusation, stating that the child has been destructive and unmanageable. What would you believe? Whom would you believe? What would you do?

Unfortunately, there often is no clear-cut way to determine whether abuse has occurred. Abuse cases typically are not easily discernible. Often, it is one person's word against another's because sufficient evidence is not available.

Due to the fact that children have very active imaginations and are creative in their play adventures, many adults tend to disbelieve their accounts of abuse. In fact, some abusers remind children of this fact in an effort to obtain their silence about the abuse. They say such things as, "No one will believe you because you are just a kid" or "Everyone knows that kids lie and make things up." As a result, many children do not talk about abusive situations, and unfortunately, many adults do not take children seriously when they do reveal an abusive relationship.

Further, many adults disbelieve reports of abuse based on the behavior and/or personality of the alleged victim. Accounts of abuse by a rebellious teen, a child with behavioral problems, or an emotionally dramatic youngster may be discounted due to the young person's problems, immaturity, or instability. What many people do not realize is that these personal problems often are manifestations of the abuse.

It should also be noted that when the alleged abuser is considered to be an outstanding member of the community, people are less likely to believe the child. In these cases, adults may assume that the child is lying because the alleged abuser is "such a nice person."

Chapter two explains that abusers are of all ages, economic groups, religious beliefs, and geographic areas. They include people of all personalities, temperaments, and dispositions. Many "nice" people are abusers. In fact, people who abuse children often are considered to be very kind and caring people.

A woman said that a wonderful man in her organization had been accused of abusing one of his children. She stated emphatically, "He said he didn't do it, and I believe him!" I responded, "Information on child abuse supports the fact that most allegations of abuse are true—whether or not they are proven in a court of law."

The director of a treatment program for abusers told me that the biggest problem she faces in treating them is denial. She explained to me that very few abusers admit their actions and that most continue to deny the accounts even after they are found guilty in court.

It is only natural for you to want to know the truth and to do what is best. But as one who works directly with children, you must not decide to report based on your personal prejudices, reactions, beliefs, investigations, or likes and dislikes. Even though you may be affected by the situation, the victim's personality, or the alleged accuser's reputation, your obligation is to the child and his or her safety. Your obligation is to report.

Why Most Accusations Are True

It Takes Courage to Talk About Abuse

When a child talks about abuse, it generally takes quite a bit of courage to do so. Perhaps the abuser threatened bodily harm to the victim, a pet, or a family member. Maybe the abuser threatened the loss of his or her love or the loss of a desired item or event, saying such things as, "I won't love you anymore if you tell," "I won't get you that bicycle you wanted," or "If you tell, Daddy will go to jail." Consequently, it would take a lot of bravery for the child to reveal abuse.

Many abuse victims fear not only what will happen, but also what others will think about them if they tell. Will people think that it was their fault? Will people think that they are lying? Will people think that they are no good? They are so overcome with fear, guilt, and shame that they are reluctant to tell anyone. Many would rather continue in the abusive relationship than confront these unwanted feelings.

For this reason, most abused children decide not to tell anyone. Those who do disclose an abusive experience are displaying courage despite their fears and feelings.

Children Seldom Make Up Stories About Abuse

It is unusual for a child to make up stories about abuse. Although children have active imaginations, their imaginations usually do not include stories of abuse. Only children who have experienced abuse have the ability to understand and explain.

"Since knowledge through observation or hearing is the basis for fantasy, children are unlikely to fantasize about sexual activity using adult terms because sexual matters are not generally discussed between parents and their children in an informative way. The child who can describe an adult's erect penis and ejaculation has had direct experience with them." (Lloyd, 1981)

"Children don't make up stories about sexual assault. Young children may have difficulty describing the incidents precisely as they occurred, complete with exact time and place. This shouldn't be cause of disbelief. Many children who are sexually assaulted may be too young to have developed those skills." (Adams and Fay, 1981)

"The thoughts behind the language of a preschooler are illogical and fantastic by adult standards, but there is a pattern to these thoughts. That pattern is forged from everyday experiences." (Tomlinson-Keasey, 1980)

In today's society, more and more young people are exposed to a variety of sexual behavior in the movies, in music videos, and in other media. Although this exposure, along with increased awareness of sexual and physical abuse, has made the younger generation more knowledgeable about these things, their stories of abuse should not be discounted.

It is imperative to remember that false stories of abuse, although they do exist, are rare. But even false accusations may indicate something described in the following sections.

Why Many False Accusations Are Revealing

Substitute Person (Transference)

There are instances in which a child accuses the wrong adult of abuse. Often, this person is one with whom the child feels safe and loved. Sometimes, however, the child chooses to blame a person whom he or she dislikes, but who is nonthreatening, as his or her substitute abuser. In these cases, the child deeply desires to reveal the abuse but remains fearful of the real abuser and what might happen to him or her for talking. In such a case, a child is telling only half the truth. The claim that the child is being abused may be true, but the identified abuser may be incorrect. The child chooses to accuse an adult with whom he or she feels safe, secure, or nonthreatened, almost as if expecting him or her to figure out the rest of the truth and tell it for him or her.

When a child talks about abuse and it becomes evident that the alleged abuser is not guilty, it is helpful to remember that the child may actually be suffering abuse—from someone else.

Substitute Accusation

Sometimes, a child says that an adult is abusing him or her or doing something that the child feels is more likely to be believed than what is actually happening. For example, a young person may report that an adult is physically abusing him or her, when, in fact, the adult is sexually abusing him or her.

To the victim, making an accusation of physical abuse is easier than revealing sexual molestation. The child feels that the substitute accusation will be better-accepted and better-understood by others.

As in the case of an accusation against a substitute person, it is important to realize that although the initial accusation may be incorrect, there may be some truth to the allegation.

Why Some Accusations Are False

Wrong (Substitute) Accusation

During a recreation program, a ten-year-old asked the staff worker if she could switch teams because she wanted to play on the same team as her friend. The recreation leader denied the request even after many appeals by the child, stating that the teams had already been selected and that the division of people into the different teams had been fair. The girl was obviously upset as she stormed away.

The next day, the recreation leader was called into the supervisor's office. The supervisor said that one of the children in the program told her parents that the leader had hit her the day before. (In this case, the parents called the program supervisor and not the local child-abuse authorities.) The staff member denied the allegations and recounted the girl's angry episode.

After further discussions among the recreation leader, the supervisor, the child, and the parents, the girl confessed that she made up the part about being struck because she was angry at the staff member. We can understand that she was angry and wanted to get back at the recreation leader, and did so by claiming that she had been physically abused. In this case, a false accusation was made. Instead of saying "You made me mad," the child said, "You hit me."

(Note: If this case had been reported to the authorities, they would have questioned the girl. It is likely that after seeing the consequences, she would have admitted making up the story, thus ending any investigation.)

False Accusation

When an allegation of abuse is determined to be false because the child gave false, incorrect, or exaggerated information, the young person should receive counseling. It is important to find out why the child provided that information and whether a substitute person or substitute accusation is involved.

Exaggerated Accusation

When exaggerated accusations occur, the alleged abusers often end up feeling like the ones who were abused. They feel victimized by their accusers. Exaggerated accusations are infrequent, but when they are made, they generally are made by adolescents.

The term "parent abuse" has come into use among parents who were falsely accused of abusing their children. Many of the alleged victims were rebellious teenagers who felt unjustly disciplined by their parents. These young people wanted more independence and fewer restrictions, and they knew about the abuse laws. They complained of emotional abuse when their parents wouldn't let them use the phone to the degree they desired or of physical abuse when they were not allowed to eat what they wanted. Such cases, however, are uncommon.

When in Doubt, Report

As was stated, there often is no clear-cut way to determine whether abuse has occurred. Even though you may feel that the child has behavioral problems, your responsibility is simply to report what you observed or were told.

Because you work directly with children, your role is to believe the child, make a report, and let the authorities determine whether the abuse occurred. Remember, you will *not* be held liable for making a report that turns out to be false, but you may be held liable for not making a report.

Reactions to Abuse

When a child "acts out" and seems to be testing your authority, or when a child is quiet and withdrawn, it helps to know that these are not unusual responses for a young person who has been abused. Along with abuse come many negative feelings, such as low self-esteem, guilt, shame, anger, and fear. These feelings manifest themselves in many ways. Often, the employees and volunteers who work with these young people are the ones who have to deal with the acting-out of these negative feelings.

This chapter presents information on the various reactions and feelings experienced by abuse victims. Not all victims respond in the same way. Some experience several reactions at the same time, whereas others focus on one. Your response to a child's reaction can be vital to his or her healing process. Although you should pay very close attention to these reactions, they are not proof of abuse; they may be indicators of other situations.

Reactions to Abuse

Eliana Gil, Ph.D. has written a small, concise, readable book titled *Outgrowing the Pain: A Book for and About Adults Abused as Children.* Gil's book addresses the various reactions, feelings, and patterns of relating to the world that abuse victims generally experience. In this highly recommended book, the author challenges the abuse victim to acknowledge what happened, even though it may be painful, and to work on being a survivor rather than a victim of the negative past. She examines four responses to abuse: denial, minimizing, rationalizing, and selective memory. We have added a fifth response: recanting.

Denial

Many people deal with unpleasant past experiences by attempting to deny the existence of these experiences. This defense mechanism protects the victim from painful memories. One of the first steps in the recovery process is to acknowledge what happened, not to deny it.

Minimizing

Some victims tend to view the abusive experiences in a way that minimizes their impact. These people make statements such as "It wasn't all that bad," "It wasn't that often," "I only had to get stitches once," or "I was only fondled, not raped." As Gil states, "The crucial aspect of the abuse is not what occurred, but what impact it had on you, how you explained it to yourself and others, and how it has affected your life." (Gil, 1983)

Rationalizing

When a victim rationalizes, he or she is either making excuses for the abuser or seeking to explain away what happened. Although there may be some contributing factors to the abuse, those factors do not excuse it or the adult's responsibility for it. Those who rationalize might be saying to themselves, "She couldn't help it; she was abused as a child, too," "He was overstressed with the family financial problems," or "They were good parents, in general."

Selective Memory

Also referred to as "blocking," selective memory occurs in a victim who finds the memories too painful and therefore begins to block them out—in a sense, to bury them. If the victim confronts the past, the memories slowly begin to emerge. This process, however, should not be forced, but be done with the help of a caring, trained professional.

Recanting

Some victims, after seeing the reactions of family members and friends, experience myriad problems associated with revealing the abuse and remember the abuser's threats. As a result, they recant their stories. They decide that telling isn't worth the emotional hurt and uncertainty, especially if some family members and friends react negatively or in disbelief. These victims may claim that they were making the whole story up and refuse to talk any further about the allegation.

In these instances, it is important to remind the person that freedom from the abuse is better than returning to the abusive situation.

Feelings About Abuse

Generally, once the victim admits the existence of the abuse, one or more of the following feelings ensues.

Fear

Those who have been abused may have received threats of harm to themselves or to loved ones, or they may have been subjected to actual physical or sexual violence. Consequently, it is not unusual for them to feel unsafe in unfamiliar surroundings or to be afraid of new people.

In one case of sexual abuse, two children were deprived of food until they performed specific sexual acts with their guardians.

As a result, they feared for their basic survival. It took months in a foster home before they began to realize that they would be given food regularly, at every meal. Until then, they ate each meal as if it were their last, consuming large amounts of food not out of hunger, but out of fear.

Guilt

Many adult abusers attribute blame to the victim—and unfortunately, children usually believe them. After all, young victims reason that if an adult told them it was their fault, the adult must know best. Therefore, the majority of abuse victims must deal with their own feelings of guilt.

One of the primary goals in counseling abuse victims is to help them realize that they were not responsible for the abuse so that they can begin unloading their tremendous guilt and feelings of responsibility.

Anger

Many abuse victims feel intense anger as they come to realize the extent to which they were violated, exploited, and betrayed. This anger may manifest itself outwardly or be turned inward, leading to further feelings of helplessness. The fact that an abuse victim feels angry is natural; it is what they do with these angry feelings that may or may not be helpful. The anger needs to be released, but it must be done in constructive, noninjurious ways.

For the victim of physical abuse, it is especially important to work through feelings of anger and to develop ways to appropriately express negative emotions. Many of these victims have seen adults display uncontrolled tempers when provoked. This increases their likelihood of repeating similar behavior.

Shame

An abused person may regret not having disclosed the abuse sooner. This person may or may not feel guilty or responsible for what happened, but he or she may feel ashamed for not revealing it in the beginning. Many victims continue to remain silent about the abuse because of their shame for not having divulged the information immediately.

One organization presented an abuse-prevention workshop for children. It was later discovered that one of the children was being abused. When asked why she didn't tell anyone about the abuse, as instructed in the workshop, she replied that she became ashamed for not having revealed the abuse sooner. These shame-ridden victims do not realize that many controlling, manipulative, and/or threatening factors were at play in the situation.

Some abuse victims also acquire what is referred to as the "damaged-goods syndrome." They feel as though they are blemished, stained, marked, scarred, or labeled. Therefore, they feel shame about their bodies, because they were treated more like objects than like human beings. Again, they should work through these deep feelings with the help of a trained professional and/or support group.

Questions Victims Ask

Common questions asked by those who have been abused include the following:

1. Why did this happen to me?
2. How will I know that it won't happen again?
3. Why me? What did I do? Did I do something wrong?
4. Why did I have to keep secrets?
5. What can I do to protect myself?
6. What if I hadn't told? What would have happened?
7. Why do I feel responsible for everything that's happened?
8. Who knows about this? Who needs to know, and who doesn't need to know?
9. What will counseling be like?
10. Why did the abuser interfere with my life?

11. Why did the abuser do what he or she did when he or she knew it was wrong?
12. Was the abuser also abused in his or her childhood?
13. Have other people been abused by this person?
14. Why did I trust the person?
15. Did anyone else know about it but didn't say anything [such as a parent]?
16. Why didn't my parent protect me when he or she saw what was happening?
17. Do other people who have been abused feel this way?
18. What will happen to the abuser?
19. Why did I let it go on so long? What was my biggest fear?
20. How can I forget about what happened?

Possible Outcomes of Abuse

Each person who has been abused is unique, and the circumstances of his or her abuse are unique. Therefore, how he or she responds to this negative experience depends on his or her feelings, personality, and situation. Following are some of the possible outcomes of abuse.

Promiscuity

Some sexually abused victims become promiscuous. They seek control over this aspect of their life and therefore engage in sex with others whom they choose, rather than being forced against their will. For some, however, the promiscuity reflects a search for the loving relationship for which they long.

One sexually abused woman whom I counseled believed that the only thing she was truly good at—the only thing in which she could take pride—was her sexual ability. She needed to understand that her promiscuity was her way of dealing with the abuse and an indication of low self-esteem and a search for self-worth.

Homosexuality

Some people who have been sexually abused, by either a member of the same gender or by a member of the opposite gender turn to homosexual relationships simply as a result of their negative experience.

A young boy who was molested by his favorite uncle may assume that this experience means that he is homosexual—because the abuse arose out of a seemingly loving relationship. A teenage girl who was forcefully molested by her older brother *and* her father may learn to hate and distrust men and to seek relationships solely with women.

Although there is some evidence that sexual abuse may cause people to question their sexual orientation, this by no means leads to the conclusion that homosexuals have necessarily been abused or will be abusers.

Trust Problems

It is easy to understand how a person who has been physically, sexually, or emotionally abused could find it hard to trust others. When trust has repeatedly been broken, a person learns to view the world and relationships as being unstable and untrustworthy. Therefore, his or her interactions with other people are based on the premise that they will be let down. This provides one of the biggest challenges for those who work with abused minors. Building trust is a long, slow process that generally is accompanied by numerous tests of character, sincerity, and genuine caring. For the older victim, the problem of trust is manifested by difficulty in developing intimacy with others.

Dependency Problems

Some victims of abuse develop an unhealthy reliance on others. In a sense, this represents the opposite of difficulty with trust, in that they trust others unquestionably, even to the extent that they believe others more than they do themselves. These people habitually defer to the preferences of others and generally do not make decisions without consulting someone.

Low Self-Esteem

The physically abused person generally has been treated as though he or she were in the way. The sexually abused person feels used — according to one victim, "like a piece of meat." The emotionally abused person is convinced of his or her uselessness. Consequently, feelings of low self-esteem run deep in the hearts and minds of those who have been abused. For many abuse victims, low self-worth is inevitable, generally leading to ongoing self-defeating behaviors.

Aggressiveness/Hostility

Many victims deal with their experiences by acting out their anger in aggressive or hostile ways. This behavior may be focused or generalized to most life situations. Often, misbehaving young people in our programs are the ones for whom we feel the least compassion. Their behavior triggers our own frustrations as we attempt to provide high-quality, orderly programs. This forces us to rise above our immediate anguish, to realize the factors involved in such conduct, to maintain our calm throughout the undesirable situation, and to choose a beneficial course of action. This is quite a challenge!

Physical Problems

Like other people, some abuse victims deal with problems by internalizing them. This method often leads to ailments such as ulcers, stomach aches, headaches, tense muscles and many other medical problems.

"Tough Skin"

As can easily be understood, many abuse victims develop tough skins as they seek to survive. These people numb their feelings, becoming unable to admit, perceive, or deal with unwanted emotions. This tough skin may be deliberate, part of an "I'm not going to let anyone hurt me" strategy, or it may slowly evolve as a way of dealing with negative experiences.

Helplessness/Depression

When a person continually is confronted by situations in which he or she feels trapped and powerless, helplessness and depression generally follow. At first, the person will struggle and search for a way out. But when repeatedly defeated, the person generally comes to believe that any attempt he or she makes to change the situation is hopeless.

Unfortunately, these feelings often carry over to life itself, and the abused person begins to feel as if he or she were in a rowboat in the open sea with no rudder or oars, at the mercy of the wind and waves. No matter what the person does, he or she feels helpless and apathetic, thinking "What's the use? Nothing will work." Such a person sees him or herself as a pawn in someone else's chess game, unable to participate in any decisions regarding his or her own destiny. These feelings commonly are accompanied by depression.

Difficulty With Boundaries

Those who have difficulty with boundaries may exhibit what is viewed as being socially inappropriate behavior. A boy who has been sexually abused, for example, may be confused as to what is appropriate behavior around older women. Or a woman dealing with an abusive past may share her story with anyone and everyone in her attempt to alleviate the painful memories—as if telling the story over and over again somehow rids her of some of the excess baggage she carries.

These people have difficulty knowing what they should and should not do or say; therefore, they often experience difficulty fitting in.

Rescues Others

Some abuse victims deal with their past by seeking to rescue others in need. These people are, in a sense, striving to give to others what they themselves need or needed. As they rescue others, they may either begin healing some of their own wounds and realize that they do not need to rescue everyone, or they burn out in the process. They become quite adept at identifying people in need and derive much self-satisfaction from being needed.

Refer also to Appendix P, "The Effects of Abuse at Different Developmental Stages," for an additional listing of possible responses.

Seeing beyond the hurts, defenses, and negative behaviors is a continual challenge for those who work with children and adolescents. The abused minors under your care need healthy role models, patience, and understanding as they learn and grow in this complicated world.

Working with Abuse Victims

*A*fter the abuse has been reported and the child or adolescent returns to your program, your actions and reactions can be crucial to his or her well-being.

Several years ago, an abused ten-year-old girl came to me for counseling, referred by the county children's protective service. She had recently moved to the area and was reassigned to me after having spent two years in individual counseling and in a support group for girls her age who had been abused.

During our first session, I asked her, "You know that the abuse wasn't your fault, don't you?" She immediately replied, "Sometimes I still think it was my fault, even though the counselors told me it wasn't." I was amazed that she still carried the burden of guilt, after two years of being told otherwise.

One of the first steps I take in working with victims of abuse is to reassure them that the abuse was not their fault. The person often responds in one of the following ways: "But I provoked my parent's anger," "But I enjoyed the sexual contact, even though I felt ashamed. It was the only time I felt loved," or "I could have been a better kid." However the victim felt about the abuse, though, it is the adult who is responsible for such behavior.

In working with children and adolescents who have been abused, your primary task is to remind them repeatedly that they were not responsible for the abuse. This chapter presents other practical suggestions for you and your staff members in working with abuse victims. Whereas chapter nine provides background on what the victims might be feeling and how they might be responding to the world, this chapter includes information on working with the abused on an ongoing basis. Some of these steps were explained elsewhere in this book but are presented here again for reference purposes.

Practical Suggestions

Encourage Victims to Get Professional Help

Whether or not the child and his or her family are already receiving outside help, it always is beneficial to reinforce the importance of such assistance. There are numerous support groups, individual and family counseling, resource agencies, and helpful materials that focus on abusive situations. Resources are listed in Appendix D. Organization and support groups are cited in Appendix E. The reading list contains recommended books.

It is important that your organization identify appropriate limits for what you can do to help. Then, when that limit is reached, get professional help.

Be Aware of Your Own Physical Gestures and Actions

A friendly touch from you could be interpreted incorrectly and result in a hindered relationship. An abused child may view "friendly" wrestling in a fearful fashion. Restrain yourself from grabbing children around the neck. You may hug a child or hold his or her hand in a friendly manner, but you first need to have an established relationship and a clear understanding of what that physical contact means. Abuse victims, like all of us, appreciate physical affirmation when it is a reflection of who they are, rather than a reflection of the other person's perverted needs, whether sexual or power-oriented.

Treat the Person with Love and Respect

Abuse victims generally feel unloved for who they are. They have been made to feel like objects, not like human beings worthy of respect and love. They need to be reminded of their individual worth. Their feelings and opinions need to be heard and encouraged as being valid and worthwhile.

Show Unconditional Love

Victims of sexual, emotional, or physical abuse generally have experienced approval and affection based on specific behavior and/or performance—that is, they have received love only on a conditional basis. They need to be shown love and acceptance no matter what they can or can't do.

Provide Examples of Healthy Relationships

Many victims of abuse have had little opportunity to observe healthy ways of relating to people. A sexually abused youth has experienced seductive behavior. A physically abused child has witnessed painful outbursts of adult anger. An emotionally abused child knows all too well that words are powerful weapons. Staff members and volunteers providing programs and services for children and adolescents can be models of positive, unconditionally caring people as they attempt to express their sexual desires, anger, and frustrations in appropriate and healthy ways.

Provide Opportunities for the Safe Release of Feelings

To assist abuse victims in the healing process, caretakers can provide a noncritical environment in which the victims can release their emotions. They need opportunities to express their feelings in a safe, supportive, nonjudgmental setting. What they need is a listening ear, not a lot of advice and recommendations. Remember, the most common feelings of abuse victims in response to the abuse are anger, guilt, shame, and fear.

Be Willing to Listen

Many abuse victims need to talk about their experience in order to gain control of and overcome their negative emotions. Your willingness to listen can help them sort out their anger, fear, and confusion. Although you may not be able to empathize personally with their experience, you can demonstrate acceptance and understanding of their trauma.

Reinforce that Revealing the Abuse was the Right Thing to Do

After revealing that they have been abused, many people experience negative reactions. Some people don't believe them, saying that they are lying. Others keep questioning their motives or asking why they didn't tell sooner.

Sometimes, when a family member is the alleged abuser, the family is torn apart. As a result, victims often wish they hadn't told and feel overly responsible for all that is happening. They need to be reminded that they were right to tell about the abuse.

Do Not Interrogate the Victim

Don't ask a victim why he or she didn't say anything sooner. Whether out of fear, responsibility, guilt, or shame, most victims feel trapped and immobilized, unable to speak out about their situation. Professionals speak of the "accommodation syndrome" when referring to the fact that many victims remain silent about the abuse. The child's low self-esteem also reinforces his or her feeling of deserving such poor treatment.

When I worked with mothers of sexually abused children, the question most asked was "Why didn't my child tell me?" It is very hard to comprehend the depth of the feelings of guilt and responsibility that most abused children experience. These feelings seem to paralyze them when it comes to telling someone about the abuse.

Respect the Victim's Privacy and Confidentiality

Allow the victim to choose when and whom to tell about his or her experience. Although it may be helpful for staff members who work directly with the child to know about the reported abuse, you must carefully consider how many staff members really need to know.

Reinforce the Fact that the Abuse Was Not the Victim's Fault

As has been mentioned several times, abuse victims must continually be reminded that it is adults who are responsible for taking care of children. When something wrong happens (such as an abusive situation), it is the adult's fault, not the child's.

Victims also need to hear that some adults do wrong things but then tell children that it is the children's fault, when it's not. You can help reinforce these important truths.

Be Prepared for Negative Behaviors

Often, abuse victims lash out at innocent others as they work through their own anger about the abuse. Their behavior may become more aggressive, abusive, negative, and inappropriate. Do not tolerate this acting-out, but seek to *lovingly* enforce the rules and regulations of your organization in dealing with incorrect behavior.

Be Prepared for a Variety of Emotions and Reactions

Common emotions and responses experienced by those who have been abused are reviewed in chapter nine. Be tolerant and prepared for these as you develop a plan for working with such reactions.

As opposed to the possible negative behaviors and acting-out, abuse victims may instead exhibit withdrawn, depressed, passive, or fearful behavior.

Encourage the Abuse Victim to Become a Survivor

Those who have been abused need to begin seeing themselves as *survivors* rather than *victims* and to be encouraged toward healing and growth. You can help them develop a positive self-image as they realize that they are human beings, worthy of respect and dignity, rather than damaged goods.

Allow time, however, for the confusion to lift and the anger to be sufficiently vented (it may take years). It can be detrimental to force abuse victims to move on before they have had adequate opportunity to work through their negative emotions.

Be A Child Advocate

You have the unique opportunity to assist greatly in the healing process due to your ongoing contact with the victims of abuse. You can be a child advocate simply by offering emotional support—be one who believes, listens, and cares unconditionally and consistently.

Programs for the Abused

Although this chapter has focused on issues related to working with abuse victims in the context of programs and services for the general population, programs specifically designed to meet the needs and concerns of abuse victims must also be addressed. More and more agencies are beginning to develop and offer activities and services for this segment of the population.

In the counseling field, for example, the number of support groups offered for abused children (and for adults who were abused as children) has increased dramatically in recent years. Some recreation agencies and child-care organizations have initiated programs and special outings for abused children. An example is Royal Family Kids Camp (RFKC).

RFKC began in 1985, when a pastor was asked to develop a summer camp program for "children less fortunate." Due to the staggering number of abused and neglected children, he decided that the camp would focus on meeting the emotional needs of these young people. The camp has grown from thirty-seven children the first year at one location to several hundred campers each summer in camps in Southern California, Idaho, Michigan, and Arizona. Largely staffed by volunteers, these weeklong camps include a "grandma and grandpa" (an older couple whose responsibilities are to love the children and give plenty of hugs), an "aunt and uncle" (who serve as positive older role models), and plenty of loving counselors (the staff-to-camper ratio generally is 1:2).

The name "Royal Family Kids Camp" reflects the founder's desire to make the children feel special and to assist in enhancing positive self-concepts (hence the word "royal"). Because RFKC is a Christian camp, the name also reminds children that they can be a part of God's "royal family." Even though not all of them may have earthly families, the children are told about their membership in God's family. The word "family" also is used to give the children a sense of belonging with the camp's staff members and the opportunity to observe, perhaps for the first time, examples of healthy family relationships.

The director reports that as a result of these camps, numerous volunteer staff have become foster parents for abused and neglected children.

This growing program (RFKC's address is listed in Appendix E) is but one example illustrating the importance of and need for programs specifically designed for abused children. Other agencies should respond to this need and develop further opportunities and services.

PART III

Working with Staff Members

▶ In working with volunteers and paid staff, four areas are of special concern to the organization's owner and/or supervisor.

▶ First, when selecting staff members, employers must minimize the risk of hiring a potential abuser; therefore, they need to know the identifying characteristics of possible child abusers.

▶ Second, staff members need to be instructed in appropriate and inappropriate behaviors.

▶ Third, every organization that works with minors should teach the young people under their care how to prevent abuse.

▶ Last, supervisors should make sure that all staff members are aware of their legal reporting responsibilities, and of the information presented in Part II of this book.

▶ These four concerns are addressed in the following chapters.

Staff Screening and Selection—Abuser Characteristics

*S*taff members of organizations that provide programs and services for children generally are selected with great care. Employers want to hire people who have experience working with children and/or adolescents and who have skills that will be beneficial to the program. With the rise in concern about child abuse, fueled by publicity about cases like the McMartin preschool case in California, employers are becoming more and more concerned about the staff screening and selection process and about the potential of hiring a possible child molester.

Are there particular traits or characteristics that may identify potential abusers? What should an employer know? How can he or she know whether an employee is an offender?

This chapter describes some of the possible traits of abusers. Very little of this information is discernible from a staff application. You will need to use other methods—the interview process and references in particular—to identify potential abusers. These methods should be used in concert.

General Characteristics of Potential Abusers

There is no way to determine whether a person is a molester from characteristics alone. The traits listed in this chapter must therefore be regarded only as guidelines for identifying potential abusers. Due to the fact that most child abusers appear to be normal and have many of the same characteristics as the general population, identifying offenders is a challenging task with an accompanying risk.

Abused as a Child

One of the best general indicators that a person is or may become an abuser is a history of childhood abuse. Although many abuse victims proclaim, "I'll never do that to my kids," a large percentage find themselves displaying similar behavior when they are under stress or their own needs aren't being met. This is how abuse is handed down from one generation to another.

Regarding sexual abuse, some studies indicate that ninety-five percent of all molesters were themselves molested as children. (Note: This does not mean that ninety-five percent of all people who have been abused will in turn abuse others, but that of those who have allegedly abused others, ninety-five percent perpetuated the cycle of abuse.)

Prior Arrests or Convictions

A person who has been arrested and/or convicted of physically or sexually abusing a child should be carefully screened before being employed. Many states allow employers to screen the police records of people who are seeking child-related employment. Further, with the written consent of the applicant, employers may request information from the law-enforcement authorities in the cities of his or her current and past residences. (This is further explained in chapter twelve.)

Characteristics of the Potential Physical and Emotional Abuser

The following characteristics apply to those who abuse others physically and/or emotionally. Information on the characteristics of sexual offenders is presented later.

Negative Attitude

Those engaged in physical and emotional abuse often display a negative attitude about life and people. Their own low self-esteem leads them to degrade others, both emotionally and physically. Not all of those who physically abuse others, however, display constant pessimism. For some, it is brought on by stressful situations and is not a continual occurrence.

Hot Temper

Many abusers would be labeled by close friends and family members as having a bad temper. They are viewed as being unable to control their anger appropriately and as reacting to negative situations with overly harsh words and actions.

Blames Others

According to most abusers, the child or some negative life situation is to blame for the abuse. "The child made me hit him," "It was his fault for provoking me," and "She didn't obey me" are statements that place blame on the victim. Whether a child is disobedient or not, he or she does not deserve to be struck or psychologically damaged. Comments such as "I can't help it; my job is stressing me out," "My husband had just yelled at me," or "I was hit when I was that age" all shift the blame. Most abusers place responsibility on the child or on other external circumstances.

The following list provides additional insight into the behavior of abusers.

Traits of the Physical Abuser

1. Has a history of abuse as child.
2. Uses harsh discipline inappropriate to the child's age and transgression.
3. Offers illogical, unconvincing explanations for what occurred (for the child's bruises, etc.).
4. Significantly misperceives child (e.g., sees him or her as a devil or monster).

5. Uses or abuses alcohol or other drugs.
6. Attempts to conceal child's injury or to protect identity of the responsible person.
7. Hits or verbally abuses child in front of others.
8. Exhibits bizarre, out-of-control behavior.

Traits of the Emotional Abuser

1. Blames or belittles the child.
2. Is cold and rejecting.
3. Withholds love.
4. Seems uninterested in child's problems.
5. Does not support, encourage, guide, or show positive behavior toward the child.
6. Has abuse in own childhood.
7. Is harsh and inflexible.
8. Ineffectively handles stress and crisis situations.
9. Has unrealistic expectations of the child.
10. Uses the child as a scapegoat.
11. Displays inconsistent and unpredictable responses.
12. Blames others and uses sarcasm.
13. Gives double messages (says one thing and does another).
14. Identifies child with a disliked person or unpleasant event.
15. Persistently ridicules the child.
16. Verbally lashes out in anger or frustration.
17. Mechanically responds to the child's needs.

Reprinted with permission from the San Francisco Child Abuse Council.

Characteristics of the Potential Sexual Abuser

Common characteristics of molesters include the following:

1. Possesses low self-esteem.

2. Blames others or circumstances rather than taking responsibility.
3. Engages in substance abuse.
4. Is skilled at manipulative behavior.
5. Desires power, control, and authority over others.
6. Displays poor impulse control ("I want what I want when I want it" mentality).
7. Relates to others immaturely socially and emotionally.
8. Is easily frustrated.
9. If married, is experiencing marital problems.

Additional characteristics, cited in *Child Molesters: A Behavioral Analysis*, (Lanning, 1987) include the following:

10. Moves frequently and unexpectedly (to avoid detection or charges).
11. Displays excessive interest in children.
12. Has an idealistic perspective of children, or may refer to them as if they were objects.
13. Seeks opportunities to be alone with children.
14. Finds legitimate access to children through employment and volunteer opportunities with children.
15. Associates primarily with children and has limited peer relationships.

Sex Offenders

Professionals in the field of sexual abuse have identified three different types of pedophiles—adults with sexual desire for children. Some of their characteristics are explained in the following section. (Note: Female pedophiles are very rare. Therefore, the pronoun "he" will be used almost exclusively in the following sections.)

Fixated Pedophiles

Fixated pedophiles usually start acting out their problems when they are thirteen or fourteen years of age. Even as adults, they are kind and gentle and think of children as their friends. In their own minds, the things they do are special favors for a child. These people lower their adult thinking to the simple levels of their victims and play childlike games with them that have sexual overtones.

Most fixated pedophiles have not had a successful adult-to-adult sexual relationship. They carefully plan their conquests and indeed get a great deal of satisfaction from the thrill of conquest.

The fixated pedophile needs more than one relationship and therefore victimizes more than one child—frequently, many children at a time. One of the greatest fears a pedophile has is that he will lose his access to children. To avoid this possibility, this person places himself in a job or volunteer position that ensures his continual access to children.

Traits of this type of child molester include the following:

1. Is very soft-spoken.
2. Is gentle.
3. Has an excellent reputation.
4. Buys things for children.
5. Does favors for children.
6. Is very neat.
7. Is very organized.
8. Spends more time with children than with adults.
9. Takes children to amusement parks, sporting events, etc.
10. Invites children to his home.
11. Finds ways to be alone with children.
12. Likes only boys or only girls, rarely both.
13. Acts adult when with parents; acts childlike when with children.
14. Associates mostly with children from single-parent homes, children whose parents are not getting along, or children with handicaps.
15. Becomes a surrogate parent to the child.
16. Frequently takes pictures and/or videotapes of children.
17. Lives alone.

Regressed Pedophiles

The regressed pedophile usually is active in the community, has no criminal record, and is well-thought-of by neighbors and friends. This pedophile likes children, probably has children, and usually spends a regular part of his time with them.

Suffering from some trauma in the past year and feeling no comfort from their current mates, regressed pedophiles start to look for comfort and reassurance from someone who is sympathetic and will not reject gentle touching and caressing. Children, their own in particular, fill the needs of regressed pedophiles.

A regressed pedophile uses his position of authority and power to scare or threaten the child into not telling. This pedophile is possessive and very jealous. He doesn't want the child to have close friends and becomes very restrictive, not allowing the child to have social contact with young people of the opposite sex.

A fixated pedophile's molestation of children is premeditated, whereas the regressed pedophile's initial offense generally is impulsive, not planned, and is precipitated by stress. While the involvements of the regressed type come and go, the fixated type exhibits persistent interest in children and displays compulsive behavior. The fixated type generally reports no history of alcohol or drug abuse, whereas the regressed molester's offenses often are alcohol-related. (Groth)

Undifferentiated Pedophiles

Fixated and regressed pedophiles love the children they molest, whereas an undifferentiated pedophile cares only about his own sexual gratification. This undifferentiated type grabs, kidnaps, and holds hostage his victims. He does not choose between boys and girls, as his only concern is to satisfy his own needs. Although most pedophiles like children of a specific age, the undifferentiated type targets those who are easy to obtain with no regard to their age.

The following chart, compiled by For Kids Sake, Inc., provides a concise summary of the behaviors and characteristics of fixated, regressed, and undifferentiated child molesters.

Understanding Pedophiles

Fixated	Regressed	Undifferentiated
	Were they victims?	
Molested as a child	Molested as a child	Molested as a child
	Their relationships	
No age-appropriate relationships	Has or has had age-appropriate relationships	Nothing but troubled relationships all ages
	Sexual orientation	
Same-sex relationships	Opposite-sex relationships	Sex with either sex
	Relationship with child	
Loving relationship with children	Loving, but power relationship with child	No love for anybody
	Approach to child	
Slow, methodical approval with bribes and favors (Candyman)	Do what I say because I know what is best for you (Chickenhawk)	Kidnaps, holds tied up, keeps captive (Pervert)
	Age preference	
Targets specific age group; 2-year difference (e.g., 3–4 years old)	Targets general age group; 5-year difference (e.g., 5–10 years old)	Targets for sexual arousal—no age preference
	Sexual contact	
Gentle, plays games, touching, rubbing, kissing, avoids penetration	Coercive, told what to do, oral copulation most common, some penetration	Tortures or injures children while having sex with them, pain heightens sexual function
	Secret	
"We don't want to get in trouble. You care about me."	"If you tell, you will get in trouble or be hurt."	Kills victim
	Time commitment	
Spends most of his time with children	Spends "special" time alone with child	Not friendly, doesn't spend time with anyone—isolated loner

Fixated	Regressed	Undifferentiated
	Access route	
Youth leader, adult babysitter, teacher	Family member, trusted care provider	Stranger
	How they think	
Psychologically lowers self to child's age	Psychologically raises child to his age	Psychologically unstable

Please remember that these characteristics are designed to provide a framework for identifying abusers. Each trait in isolation may be meaningless. These traits must be considered in conjunction with other characteristics before being used to label a person.

Female Sexual Offenders

Although most cases of molestation involve male offenders, there also are female offenders. One researcher estimated that five percent of boy and twenty percent of girl victims are molested by females (Finklehor, 1984). Some of these offenders are the primary and only initiators of sexual behavior, while others may have participated in sex acts with children along with a male partner. Here are the profiles of several possible types of female sexual offenders.

Delayed Adolescent Sexual Curiosity
Characteristics:

1. She married young.
2. She was reared in a very strict home.
3. Her family was/is very religious.
4. Her husband is gone frequently.
5. Her husband is not very supportive.
6. She is sexually naive and immature.

This type of offender did not have the opportunity for normal experimentation with the opposite sex during adolescence, and her sexual experiences are limited to those with her husband. If he is domineering and she is too afraid to try anything different, her sexual curiosity may not have been satisfied. Thus, she experiments on her own child. This inappropriate sexual contact starts out as experimentation but develops into a closeness she has never known, which is reinforced by a gentle, caring, tender child.

The mother may achieve sexual gratification from the child's body lying next to hers, from rubbing her body against that of the child's, from digital penetration, or from mutual masturbation.

Mother and Child Used for Sexual Stimulation
Characteristics:

1. The mother is very dependent on the father figure.
2. The mother frequently is the victim of physical abuse.
3. The mother is afraid of the father figure.
4. The mother has a low self-image.
5. The father figure exaggerates his masculinity in dress, work, and with his peers.
6. The father usually has drug or alcohol problems that have affected his sexual performance.

In this type of sexual misuse, the mother and the child are victimized, used as stimulators to help the father get an erection or achieve orgasm. The mother and child may undress and frolic in front of the father figure, may simulate sex acts, or may actually perform sex acts with each other or with the male adult. In some rare instances, the mother may actually assist the male by holding the child or by performing sexual acts with both the child and adult.

Women Who Molest for Profit
Characteristics:

1. She usually is a prostitute who uses her own child for monetary gain.
2. She can be a single parent forced into working to support herself and her child, with no job skills other than child care, and may be in a desperate financial circumstance that needs a quick solution.

3. She may have a drug addiction and need money to finance it.

A *Los Angeles Times* article suggested that approximately twenty percent of men who engage prostitutes ask whether they know of or have a child available for sex. Prostitutes supposedly receive three-hundred percent more for the sexual use of their children than they can for selling their own bodies.

Our society's emphasis on money and on making it "quick and easy" has affected the number of children used both as prostitutes and for kiddie pornography (magazines and videos). Testimony before the Meese Commission on Pornography (1986) suggests that kiddie pornography by itself is a $2 billion per year industry.

The Child as a Non-Threatening Lover

Characteristics:

1. The mother is lonely.
2. The father is gone for long periods.
3. The father works nights.
4. The mother has not had much tenderness in her life.

In these cases, the mother either is alone (divorced, widowed) or has a husband who frequently is gone or works nights. The lonely nights may set up a pattern in which the child sleeps with the mother for closeness and warmth; this may lead to sexual experimentation and misuse by the parent. The child gives the adult the closeness, warmth, and tenderness she needs without demands, thus becoming a non-threatening, non-demanding lover.

Again, there is no way to determine whether a person is a molester from characteristics alone. The traits listed in this chapter must therefore be regarded only as guidelines for identifying potential abusers.

Staff Selection— The Application, Interview, and References

*G*iven the previous chapter's information, the employer may now take into consideration the various characteristics and behaviors exhibited by abusers while reviewing applications, conducting interviews, and checking the references of prospective staff members. Caution must be taken, however, that the organization follow state and federal laws and regulations on information obtained on the employment form, during the interview, or from a reference.

Again, very little *character* information is discernible from an application form. You will need to use other methods, including the interview and references, to help in your appraisal of potential staff members.

Many of the questions you should be asking may not be different from the questions you already are asking. You need, however, to learn to listen differently to the answers—to listen for possible characteristics of abusers.

The Application

The application form can provide helpful information in the initial screening of prospective employees. Information regarding previous residences may identify a person who has moved frequently and unexpectedly. Information on dates and types of employment may reveal unexplained gaps or reasons for termination. A listing of extracurricular or volunteer experiences can be examined to ascertain whether the applicant engages in any activities with peers or whether his or her involvements are solely with children. (Appendix F includes a sample employment form that can be adapted for various organizations' needs.)

Depending on state legislation, the application form may include a section for written consent (authorization) to check any criminal records. Many states provide employers access to criminal records so that they can screen applicants for jobs working with young people. Any applicant with a record of child abuse, physical or sexual, should be disqualified. (See Appendix G for an example of an authorization to check criminal records.)

A completed application is the first screening tool for a potential position, volunteer or paid. Those who do not answer all required questions of the application should not be considered.

The Interview

The employment interview generally is the most effective means of staff selection. It gives the employer an opportunity to observe the applicant's mannerisms, body language, eye contact, and appearance and to further clarify items on the application form. It also provides an opportunity to ask key questions that may reveal helpful information about the applicant's attitudes toward work and people.

During the interview, the employer must evaluate the technical expertise and experience of the applicant in order to determine whether he or she possesses the needed skills or is trainable. Information on the application should be clarified, amplified, and verified. The employer also must decide whether the applicant's disposition is suitable for the position for which he or she has applied.

During the interview, the employer must keep in mind the various warning signs that might indicate a tendency toward child abuse. It is also suggested that applicants be informed of the agency's concern about the safety of its clientele and of the fact that any activity that harms a child, intentionally or not, will not be tolerated. Some abusive adults show a lack of control regarding child issues, and some molesters seem to boast about how wonderful they are with children. They may even show signs of sexual stimulation when asked about personal contact with children. The most desirable employee is not one who devotes one-hundred percent of his or her time to children, but one who seems to have a balanced life with regard to contact with children and adults.

The American Camping Association offers a one-page technical information paper (TIP) on interview guidelines for camp directors. It includes the four major mistakes made during employment interviews that limit effectiveness. If these problem areas are avoided, the employer will afford him or herself a better opportunity to evaluate and observe, directly and indirectly, potential areas of concern. It is a mistake for the employer to do any of the following things:

1. *Talk too much.* Because people in managerial positions are, by nature of their personalities, very articulate and feel more comfortable when they are in command of a situation, this probably is the most-often-made mistake. Two-way communication is almost impossible in this situation, and there is no opportunity to gather impressions or to form opinions about the interviewee.
2. *Jump to conclusions.* Based on a single fact, interviewers can reach a conclusion that may be erroneous.
3. *Phrase questions in such a way as to suggest the desired response.* A question such as "Did you take part in extracurricular activities in college?" cues the applicant that this is important, and he or she begins to search his or her experience for a favorable response. A more general question—for example, "Tell me about your college experience; what did you find particularly helpful?"—generally elicits the desired information. The omission of information about extracurricular

activities may indicate that the applicant was not involved.

4. *Fail to translate facts into on-the-job behavior.* For instance, you have noted the fact that the applicant's favorite subject was science. That fact does not translate into job behavior if science is not part of the requirement of the job . . . unless, in pursuing the question, you find that the interviewee liked science because there was always a right answer—and only one answer. This reply, correctly translated, may tell you something about the kind of job environment in which he or she will function well.

Several other mistakes happen less frequently but create additional problems. Those mistakes are as follows:

1. Permitting one trait, favorable or unfavorable, to influence the interviewer's thinking and impressions in other areas—for example, attributing general positive qualities to an applicant on the basis of his or her verbal ability or appearance.
2. Oversimplifying—expressing complicated behavior traits in simple terms.
3. Making impulsive conclusions in simple terms—drawing opinions from inadequate data. An example would be assuming that a successful counselor will make a successful administrator.
4. Pre-judging—reaching a final or near-final conclusion before interviewing the applicant.

Interview Questions

Questions asked during an interview should be designed to obtain the desired information. Some questions, therefore, must be open-ended; others need to be specific and closed. The interviewer also must remember to guard against phrasing questions in such a way as to imply a desired response. Using case studies (for example, asking, "What would *you* do in this situation?") during the interview also is recommended.

The questions chosen and how they are phrased can greatly assist the employer in identifying potential problem areas. Key questions might include the following:

1. Briefly summarize your employment history. Which of your previous positions do you think will be most helpful in this job? What did you like best/least about that position? What did you like/dislike about your supervisor? Do you feel that you were effective in that position? Would you do anything differently?
2. What do you consider to be your strengths? Your weaknesses? How would you describe yourself? How would a friend describe you? How would a past employer describe you?
3. Why do you want to work with children? With what age group and which gender do you prefer to work? How do you deal with discipline problems? Given the following situation [provide a common scenario], what would you do?
4. How do you deal with stress? How do you deal with interpersonal problems?

References

Most employers require at least three references from friends and past employers, and people not related to the applicant, who have known him or her for several years. It is helpful to obtain information from references on the nature of their relationship with the applicant and how long they have known the applicant.

It also is helpful to get a reference's name, position, address, and phone number. The latter information is especially important when a phone call is needed to further clarify the candidate's character and experience.

Some organizations routinely contact references by phone.

Often, these reference checks include personal references as well as those from previous employers and/or teachers. Phone conversations inevitably provide helpful information not contained in the reference forms.

In conducting phone reference checks, an employer seeks to find out more about the character and work habits of the applicant. These checks also afford the employer the opportunity to determine whether any information given on the application or during the interview differs from that obtained during the phone calls.

Key questions to ask past employers could include the following: "Would you hire this person again?," "How would you describe this person's character?," "What were the person's strengths and weaknesses, especially in regard to working with children?," "Would you hire this person to care for your own children, if you have any?," and "Are there any problems that might interfere with this person's ability to work effectively with children?"

Although most past supervisors are willing to answer questions, some organizations refer all reference checks to the personnel office. This is especially true in states where past employer statements have been challenged in court. These organizations provide information only to inquisitive future employers—information such as whether the person worked at their organization, his or her job responsibilities, and his or her dates of employment.

Since the references provided by applicants are generally people who have something positive to say, it may also prove helpful to ask for the names of other people who know or have worked with the applicant.

Staff screening and selection are among the most important responsibilities of any employer, due to the fact that the quality of service provided, the clients' safety, and the reputation of the agency are determined by the caliber of the staff members. Therefore, the extra time and care you take in selecting employees and in familiarizing yourself with the characteristics of potential abusers is time well-spent.

Staff Training

*T*he importance of staff training cannot be overstated. It is during this time that staff members receive what the owner, administrator, or director considers to be most valuable to the successful implementation of the service or program. The initial training period may be the employer's only opportunity to present topics fully. In training sessions, concentration usually is maximized and distractions are minimized.

Staff training must include information on appropriate and inappropriate staff behavior; laws, regulations, and safety; and background information about the organization, its philosophy, and its goals. In organizations that serve children and adolescents, staff training may include program-skill development, such as games, music, arts and crafts, and outdoor living.

The type of agency, the demands placed on it, its location, its size, the type of clientele it serves and the experience of its staff members, affect the choice of topics to be covered during staff training. The amount of time allotted to various training topics generally reflects the organization's priorities.

An agency that spends extra time on safety guidelines, first aid, and emergency procedures is stating its belief in the importance of safety. An organization that only briefly reviews required written reports and has no established method of follow-up on its documentation procedures is indirectly stating its lack of commitment to these issues.

Commitment

The inclusion of information on child abuse should not be viewed as optional but as essential for the staff training agenda. All staff members must be apprised of their responsibilities under the state reporting laws and the agency's policies. They also should be familiar with possible indicators of abuse and must know the established procedures to follow in the event of an occurrence, suspicion, discovery, or accusation of abuse. Agency policies and procedures on suspicion of and reporting of abuse should be presented to all staff members.

With growing public concern about child abuse, the decision to include information on this topic in training should be clear. How much time to allot to this topic, however, is not as clear.

Some organizations that have only three days of staff training may schedule an entire day for the presentation of child-abuse information. Others, with a week or more of training time, may give only a half-hour to the topic. Although many factors must be considered, when little or no time has been allotted to child abuse, that fact reflects either the agency's lack of awareness or its lack of commitment to deterring this overwhelming problem.

Guidelines for Staff Training

Who Should Present

If possible, it would be beneficial to have as a guest speaker a representative of the local child-protective service, social-service agency, or child-welfare agency who works directly with child-abuse cases or a therapist who specializes in counseling abuse victims. This contact may prove to be valuable when you find yourself in need of a professional opinion. It would, of course, be additionally valuable to have a contact who already is familiar with your agency.

If, however, a professional involved in the field of child abuse is not available, it is possible for someone in your organization to present this topic with the help of this book.

What to Present

The following sections contain sample outlines that can be used in preparing training presentations on child abuse. These outlines may be given to the guest speaker or used by someone in the agency who will be involved in the training.

It is important to provide information on the indicators of abuse so that staff members are aware of and will be able to recognize symptoms and behaviors (chapter five). State laws and reporting requirements (chapter six) must be presented, as well as what steps should be taken when abuse has been revealed or is suspected, or when an accusation has been made (chapter seven). Other topics to include are the organization's policies on interaction with clientele, abuse prevention (chapter fourteen), and documentation procedures (chapter fifteen).

It is essential to go over the actual forms and written reports with staff members who are required to maintain such records. These forms, listed in chapter fifteen, include an official state child-abuse reporting form, a mandated-reporter acknowledgment form (not required in all states), an accident report form, a supplemental child-abuse report form, and an incident-report form.

If additional time is available, it is helpful to provide a historical perspective on abuse (chapter two) and information on the factors that contribute to abusive situations and relationships (chapter four). The presentation also could include a discussion of how victims reveal and react to abuse (chapter eight and nine) and how staff members can be sensitive and helpful to those who have been abused (chapter ten).

Training Outline 1

I. Child Abuse Awareness

Discuss the importance of knowing about and being aware of child abuse, as well as the reasons for becoming involved in abuse prevention (chapter one).

II. Understanding Abuse

  A. Prevalence—how widespread is abuse?

  There are more than two million cases of serious child abuse reported every year in the United States. One of every three to four females and one of every seven males have reported being sexually molested (chapter one).

  B. Demographics—is there a pattern of abuse or with abusers?

  There is no pattern. Child abuse occurs in all socioeconomic, ethnic, and age groups and in all geographic areas (chapter two).

  C. Historical perspective—how long has abuse been happening?

  The maltreatment of children began because they were regarded as property. Many adults took seriously the religious mandate to not spare the rod. Eventually, the Society for the Prevention of Cruelty to Children was formed (chapter two).

  D. Who abuses?

  Generally, the abuser is someone the child knows—a relative, babysitter, family friend, family member, teacher, coach, institutional or agency employee (chapters two and three).

  E. What contributes to abusive situations and relationships?

   1. Historical or background indicators

   The abuser also was abused; family violence and/or substance abuse exists; and there is a lack of education, experience, and training in child care (chapter four).

    2. Situational factors

The likelihood of abuse increases as the following are present: extreme parental stress, social isolation, delay in parent-infant bonding, resentment of a specific child, poor housing, marital problems, financial problems and/or unemployment, and unexpected life crises (chapter four).

    3. Personality factors

The likelihood of abuse increases as a person manifests the following characteristics: has unrealistic expectations, controls his or her anger poorly, feels rejected, displays a poor self-image, and/or is depressed (chapter four).

F. What are the types of abuse?

The different types of abuse (chapter three) are as follows:

    1. Physical
    2. Sexual
    3. Neglect
    4. Emotional

III. Indicators of Abuse

A. Physical signs and symptoms (chapter five).

B. Behavioral signs and symptoms (chapter five).

C. Developmental signs and symptoms (chapter five).

IV. Employee Responsibilities

A. Staff policies, guidelines, and behaviors—appropriate and inappropriate.

State the rules and policies of your agency (chapter fourteen).

B. State child-abuse laws: you are a mandated reporter.

Refer to chapter six for information on the child-abuse laws and the reporting requirements.

C. What, how, when and where to report.

Reporting (generally by phone *and* in written form) all revealed or suspected cases of abuse to the local authorities, as required by each state (chapter six).

  D. Organizational procedures.
  Present the steps that your agency or organization follows given a revealed or suspected incident of abuse (chapter seven).

  E. Documentation requirements.
  Explain and demonstrate how to complete the various forms and reports (chapter fifteen).

  V. Reactions to Abuse
  Review the possible reactions, accusations, feelings, and outcomes experienced by abuse victims (chapters eight and nine).

  VI. Working With Abuse Victims
  Review the list of suggestions for being sensitive to and helping the abuse victim (chapter ten).

Training Outline 2—Short Version

  I. Introduction and Background Information (brief)
  A. Discuss the importance of knowing about child abuse (chapter one).
  B. If time permits, present a brief summary of the prevalence, background, and causes of abuse (chapters one, two, and four).
  C. Briefly explain the different types of abuse (chapter three).
  1. Physical
  2. Sexual
  3. Neglect
  4. Emotional

  II. Possible Indicators of Abuse
  A. Physical signs and symptoms (chapter five).
  B. Behavioral signs and symptoms (chapter five).

C. Developmental signs and symptoms (chapter five).
III. Employee Responsibilities
    A. Staff policies, guidelines, and behaviors—appropriate and inappropriate (chapter fourteen).
    B. State child-abuse laws: what, how, when and where to report (chapter six).
    C. Organizational procedures (chapter seven).
    D. Documentation requirements (chapter fifteen).

How to Present

As is true of any presentation, it is important to keep a training session interesting in order to maximize the amount of material participants will retain. Following are a few suggestions:

1. Use a well-lighted room or outdoor location with a comfortable temperature.
2. Plan the session during a time of day when staff members generally are most willing to sit and listen to a presentation (i.e., in the morning).
3. Allow for diversity in the presentation. Use lectures, discussions, case studies and stories, audiovisuals (charts, videos, films), hands-on projects (such as practicing how to write reports and required documents), role-playing, and other methods of instruction. This serves to acknowledge the diversity of the employee's learning styles and helps keep the session interesting.

    Several stories are included in this book; additional case histories are presented in Appendix H. Actual stories provide concrete examples that people generally remember longer than they do statistics.
4. Reinforce the participant's learning. For example, assign homework, develop discussion or support groups, divide the session into two parts, and/or provide a summary at the end and beginning of each subtopic.

Resources

Various resources for staff training are listed in Appendix D. This list includes videos, films, and other helpful materials on training employees and volunteers to deal with child abuse.

Precautions and Prevention

During an outing to a public swimming area, one of the children, while going to the bathroom, was grabbed by a man and pulled into one of the stalls in the men's restroom. The child was fondled and also forced to touch the man's genitals before being let go. What steps might have been taken beforehand to help deter an incident like this? What would you have done?

This chapter addresses both what precautions those working with young people can take and what steps can be taught to children and adults to guard against the occurrence of abuse. Steps are given to help providers minimize the potential of abuse occurring within their program and to maximize the organization's effectiveness in preventing abuse of those under their care. The difference between discipline and abuse also is addressed in this chapter.

For Those in Charge—Precautions and Preventions

Owners, directors and supervisors must be keenly aware of their need to use certain precautions to ensure the health and safety of the minors under their care.

Become Informed

All those in professions providing direct service to young people need to be acquainted with the problems, issues, and reporting laws pertaining to child abuse, as well as the behavioral indicators in both the abused individual and the offender. Reading this book demonstrates your desire to accomplish this step.

Meet the Local Authorities and Professionals

When you have questions and/or concerns, it is easier to call the local authorities if you have met or spoken with them previously. It is better to establish a relationship beforehand than in the midst of a crisis. Whenever a question regarding abuse arises, it is comforting to know you have a resource person to call.

Select Your Staff Carefully

The extra time taken in checking references and criminal records may, in the end, save your program from being closed due to an accusation of abuse against a staff member. Chapters eleven and twelve provide guidelines and suggestions for staff screening and selection procedures, as well as information on identifying potential abusers.

Thoroughly Train All Staff Members

Chapter thirteen provides essential information on staff training. This training should include both full-time and part-time staff members as well as volunteers. Program operators and directors also should consider training support-staff members and program-staff members. When staff members are educated about child abuse and aware of their responsibility for prevention, reporting, and safety, the director can breathe easier.

Staff training cannot be underestimated. It can deter potential offenders, encourage abused staff members to work through their own negative pasts, and assist in the identification and prevention of abuse.

Examine Your Program

Identify situations in which abuse might occur, then establish policies as needed.

In the example given at the beginning of the chapter, in which the child was molested by someone during an outing, the program could have developed one of the following policies:

1. Participants are not allowed to go anywhere without a partner.
2. Participants must be accompanied by an adult when using public facilities.
3. Participants must receive permission before leaving the group.

Identify which activities might provide opportunities for abuse, not just by outsiders, but also by employees. Are there activities in which a staff member is alone with a child for long periods? What policies do you have that reflect commitment to safety and abuse prevention? How are those policies communicated to staff?

Observe Staff Members' Interactions with Children

With the list of characteristics and behaviors presented in chapter eleven, you now are better equipped to identify potential problems among paid and volunteer staff members. You are not on a witch hunt, but simply need to be aware of the possible behaviors and characteristics that may indicate abuse.

The plan for supervising staff members should include regular opportunities to observe them interacting with children. Specific training should be provided to staff members who have supervisory responsibility for other employees. Supervisors must be able to identify and address inappropriate staff behavior that may be a result of immaturity, inexperience, stress, poor judgment, or lack of knowledge.

For Staff Members—Precautions and Preventions

As one who works with children, you potentially are vulnerable to charges of sexual or physical abuse. Following are some precautions to help deter accusations.

Always Be in View of Others

If you need to meet with a young person alone, do so in a place that is well away from the ears of others, but in view. For example, in the camp setting, you might go to the end of the swimming pier. In the recreation program, go outside the gym (where people come and go) or at the end of the athletic field. In the child-care center, go outside to the play yard, but remain in view from the windows. Try not to use private rooms with the doors shut.

Do Not Allow Program Participants into Private Staff Areas

Especially in the resident-camp setting and with child-care programs located in private homes, it is not wise to let anyone visit the private quarters of adult staff members. When more than two adults will be present, visitation may be granted, depending upon the rules of the organization.

Have a Set Procedure for Handling Discipline

If all staff members follow established procedures for discipline, procedures that have been posted and provided to parents, the likelihood of an accusation of physical abuse will be minimized. Later in this chapter information is presented that helps clarify the sometimes fine line between discipline and abuse.

Be Aware of What You Share

Young people are naturally curious and often ask staff members personal questions about relationships, dating, and sexual activity.

It is not unusual for the children and adolescents under your care to develop crushes on a staff member. These feelings, along with the curiosity, often are accompanied by a wild imagination and personal fantasies. Therefore, it is important to use discretion in what you share with the youth and to avoid details when discussing sensitive issues or your private life.

You should be aware not only of what you share, but also of what you ask. Do not ask a youth personal questions regarding sexual experiences.

Report and/or Record Suspicious or Unusual Observations

Staff members who notice any unusual behavior or suspicious activities should make note of it and tell their supervisor. In most cases, there are no repercussions, but this is an important precaution if it is later determined that you observed questionable conduct and did not report or record it.

In rare instances, you may be the one accused of causing or contributing to the problems. That is, a parent accused of abusing his or her child may say that the child began to exhibit these indicators of abuse after enrollment in your program. If you also observed these initial behavioral concerns and documented them, you will stand on firmer ground against any accusations made against you and your agency. (Note: The following chapter addresses the need for documentation before, during, and after unusual behavior is observed or abuse is suspected.)

Supervise Private Activities in Pairs

During a swimming outing, an overnight trip, or a residential camp session, there often are situations in which those involved must change clothes, put on bathing suits, or take showers. During these times, it is best to have the children supervised by more than one staff member who is of the same gender as the children.

Do Not Force Yourself on a Minor

Those who work with young people are understandably drawn to a shy or discouraged child in the hope of helping him or her. This must be done, however, in a way that respects the child and his or her level of comfort with physical and emotional displays of affection.

Discipline vs. Abuse

For parents and for care providers, the line between discipline and abuse is not always clearly drawn. What one person may consider abuse, another may consider firm discipline.

The San Francisco Child Abuse Council has developed a helpful chart explaining the differences between discipline and abuse for those who live and/or work with children.

Discipline	Abuse
### Defined	### Defined
A positive method of training a child toward self-control and self-confidence.	Chronic or persistent maltreatment of a child by an adult through fostering external controls.
### Characteristics	### Characteristics
Encourages the child to learn socially acceptable behavior and ways of expressing his or her natural desires and drives.	Promotes increasingly self-destructive, socially deviant, and/or violent behavior.
Helps the child positively shape future behavior.	Satisfies the adult's needs while imposing socially unacceptable control on the child.
Enhances the child's sense of self-worth and pride in his or her abilities.	Generates feelings of shame or guilt, which are destructive to the child's self-image.
Teaches healthy independence.	Makes it difficult for the child to form lasting relationships.
Is learned by example.	Promotes low self-esteem, feelings of inadequacy, and self-rejection.
### Discipline Fails When	Fosters unhealthy dependency.
The technique or approach used does not change with the developmental level and changes of the child.	Is perpetuated generationally.
	### Abuse Is Prevented When
The child's positive aspects consistently are ignored.	Children are supported in developing positive self-images.

Discipline	Abuse
Discipline Fails When	***Abuse Is Prevented When***
Communication between adults and children breaks down.	Children are not exploited by adults.
Adults place unrealistic demands, expectations, or limits on children.	The rights of children to healthy, happy lives are recognized and actively supported.
Adults fail to meet their own needs and desires regularly, through healthy and appropriate channels.	Adult-child communication patterns remain open, clear, positive, and consistent.
	The demands placed on children realistically parallel their physical, mental, and emotional capabilities.

Abuse Prevention for Parents and Staff Members

The fine line between discipline and abuse often can be widened by following some of the following practical tips on working with children.

1. Don't discipline children when you are upset. Doing so may lead to your speaking emotionally damaging words or using harsh physical punishment. Take a few moments to calm down and objectively evaluate the situation before disciplining.
2. Try to see life from a child's perspective.
3. Learn as much as you can about the growth and development of children, and seek to creatively apply this knowledge to your work with children.
4. Appreciate the child's individuality and encourage its healthy development.
5. Strive for fairness, consistency, and realistic limit-setting with children.
6. Develop a personal support system of understanding peers. It helps to be able to share with others who are in the same situation.
7. Expand your horizons to include outside interests. Spend time and energy doing things you enjoy.

8. Develop a positive attitude and a good sense of humor.
9. De-stress yourself by taking time out to regularly re-energize.
10. Actively seek out and use community resources for help in solving personal or work-related problems.

Reprinted by permission from the San Francisco Child Abuse Council.

For Children—Prevention Ideas and Skills

The Child Abuse Prevention Program (CAPP) in Santa Cruz, California, provides training to children, parents, and to those working with minors. The program's goal is to prevent abuse by educating both children and those who live or work with them. Following is a list of some of CAPP's suggestions for the prevention of child abuse.

1. Make sure children have as much good, appropriate touching in their lives as possible. They'll be less vulnerable and less willing to put up with inappropriate touches.
2. Give children opportunities to make decisions about their bodies so that they know they have the right to determine how their bodies will be touched. For example, if a child doesn't feel comfortable with an adult's means of affection, support his or her decision to refuse it.
3. Let children know that it is all right to trust their intuition or "uh-oh" feelings. They don't have to stick around and be polite (even to adults) if they feel that something is wrong.
4. Keep communication lines with children open so that they feel they can come to you for help.
5. Make sure young children know the correct names for private body parts so that they don't feel that these parts are unmentionable.

6. Repeatedly tell children that they are never to blame if they have been sexually abused, even if they consented out of a need for affection. It is always the adult's (or older child's) fault.

7. Instead of using "bad" touching when referring to sexual abuse, use "secret" or "confusing" touching. Abusers usually make the child feel like a partner rather than a victim. Therefore, if the child hears that this kind of touching is bad, he or she may conclude that he or she is bad and will be less likely to report what has happened.

8. Play the "What if . . . ?" game. This is a game you can play with children to help them brainstorm about what they would do in dangerous situations. Having a plan is an important method of reducing a child's vulnerability to assault.

   The game is played by asking the child, "What would you do if . . . ?" and then letting the child respond. The key is to let children come up with ideas and then reinforce their good ideas with praise and approval. This will empower them by building their self-confidence. Some questions you can ask are:

   a. "What if you were waiting to be picked up, and someone you didn't know said that you were supposed to go with them? What would you do?"

   b. "What would you do if an adult did something to you, or had you do something, that you didn't like or that you didn't understand, and asked you to keep it a secret?"

9. Tell stories about children staying safe in any number of potentially dangerous situations (getting lost, being with strangers, physical or sexual abuse). Always end with a successful way of dealing with the situation.

10. Teach children what bribes and bad favors are and what the difference is between good and bad secrets (i.e., birthday presents vs. abuse).

CHAPTER FOURTEEN

11. Teach children when it is appropriate to say, "No!" Many children learn that they are not supposed to talk back to adults or to refuse to do anything they are told.

12. Encourage games and organized sports for both boys and girls. This will help them gain a sense of physical self-confidence and minimize feelings of powerlessness if they are assaulted. Teach them to kick and run if an adult forces them to do something that they know is wrong.

13. Discuss children's rights: the right not to be touched in ways that make them feel uncomfortable, the right to say "No", and the right to get help.

Additional information on child-abuse prevention is provided in Appendix I.

Documentation—
A Safeguard

A child-care worker finds herself in a potentially harmful situation. Fortunately, she remembers the organization's policy on what actions she should take to ensure the children's safety.

A recreation leader responds to a negative event by following the procedures outlined during staff training and contacts the appropriate people.

Both these people knew what to do because the agencies for which they work had documented specific policies and procedures to follow and had thoroughly trained staff members in their implementation.

In one resident summer camp, a camper fell out of his top bunk. Although the child appeared to be fine, the counselor knew that he should take the boy to see the nurse even though it was the middle of the night. The nurse checked the child, noting her findings, concerns, and recommendations; sent the camper back to his cabin; and asked him to come see her in the morning before breakfast. The next morning, he came to visit; she felt that he would be fine and sent him on to enjoy the day's regular activities. She once again noted the visit and her treatment decision in the medical record book. Additionally, the cabin counselor completed one of the camp's incident-report forms, explaining what had happened, and gave it to the camp director.

Upon the child's arrival back home, the parent noticed bruises on the child's head and made a report to the local child-abuse agency. When the authorities came to the camp, the director was able to show the nurse's documentation and adequately explain the marks. Charges were not filed, and the investigation was dropped.

The importance of documentation cannot be understated. Every organization must develop and document policies regarding young people under its care as well as what procedures staff members should follow in the event of an undesirable event, such as abuse. Further, agencies should require documentation of all incidents involving children.

The purposes of documentation are twofold: to ensure the safety of the participants, and to provide the agency with evidence it can use when reporting abuse or being accused of abuse. With regard to the latter purpose, documentation protects you and the agency from false accusations of abuse and can also provide important information to officials investigating a report.

Document Policies and Procedures

Every agency that serves children needs to develop policies that are designed to address the safety of participants in its programs. Procedures must be established and followed that identify the steps to be taken in an emergency or matter of legal concern.

Unfortunately, many organizations have written plans but do not follow them, or have inadequate plans, or have no written plans at all. All situations involving safety or legal concerns are best dealt with when written policies and procedures delineate the steps to be taken.

Developing Policies

The first step in developing a written policy on potentially harmful situations is to list all the possible incidents that might reasonably occur in your agency, given its location, its staffing (part-time, volunteers, teenagers, etc.), and its program. It might be helpful to gather information from other, similar organizations regarding their policies for dealing with and preventing abuse.

The second step is to inform the staff members of the policies. Make sure that all staff members know the policy on being alone with a child, on undressing, on participants' presence in staff areas, and on the limits of discipline.

The third step is to make sure that the policies are being implemented. Written plans alone do not prevent harmful situations from occurring. In the earlier example about the child who was molested while using the public restroom during a swimming outing, the agency may in fact have had a policy similar to one of those listed. But if one did exist, it wasn't followed.

Developing Procedures

What steps will you follow in dealing with the child about whom you just filed a report of suspected abuse? What plan of action will you take when you or someone in your agency has been accused of abuse? Most agencies have a crisis-management plan for dealing with some physical danger (such as fire, earthquake, tornado, and drowning), but neglect to include a plan of action on dealing with an abuse crisis.

One agency has a crisis-management plan that includes the following information:

1. A listing (in order of priority, with names and phone numbers) of those on the "crisis team".
2. A listing (with names and phone numbers) of those on the "contact list".
3. The name and phone number of the person responsible for media relations.

The *crisis team* should include the organization's media contact person and the names of those who are trained in the area of abuse—generally, the supervisors of the organization. Members of the crisis team must clarify the communication procedures that will be needed before they are needed. When a report is filed following an accusation against the organization, will the parent(s) be called by someone in the organization, and if so, by whom? Which other staff members would need to know about the situation, and who should be the one to tell them?

The *contact list* may include a physician, psychologist, or social worker; the local child-abuse authorities; the organization's insurance company; and the organization's attorney. This list may also include groups of people to be notified in certain situations, such as parents of other children in the program.

Someone in the organization—an employee, owner, or board member—should be designated to serve as a *media contact* in the event that public attention is drawn to the incident.

Camp Quaker Heights in Iowa states, "It is important that only one person speak on behalf of the organization regarding any situation to eliminate any rumors or false information being given out which could be damaging or inflate the situation out of proportion. Therefore, all media inquiries will be directed to the spokesperson only."

Ashmen and Mattocks (*Journal of Christian Camping*, July/August 1984) not only encourage the designation of a spokesperson, but also recommend that organizations establish a media file that includes the names and numbers of key media representatives. They further state that printed background data on the program or agency could be given to (and would be appreciated by) media representatives. They add, "In dealing with the media, you should always try to provide a quick and honest response to requests for information. If you try to block any coverage or investigation, the information will most likely be obtained in spite of you, and you will be resented for your lack of cooperation." When you provide information to the media, it is important to consider what is best for the children and parents involved.

Dealing With Parents

Any crisis-management plan should include a policy that specifies when and how parents should be notified. If an accusation is made against a staff member, the policy may specify that parents of all participants in that staff member's group must be notified. An organization that does not notify parents of participants in such a situation may find itself in danger of other civil law-suits for *failure to warn*.

The person or people responsible for contacting parents should have training, based on recommendations from child-abuse authorities and legal counsel, on what information should and should not be given to parents. Parents will need reassurance that all possible steps are being taken to protect their children and that established routines and programs are being continued.

Last, the plan should clarify what paperwork and documentation is required and who is responsible for completing it.

Unfortunately, in far too many instances, people do not follow established procedures and guidelines. This is generally due to the fact that they forgot those procedures (remember the importance of thorough, effective training and practice!) or in the haste of the moment, decided to implement their own plan. Staff members must not only effectively learn the organization's policies and guidelines on what actions are to be taken and when, but also must follow them.

The documentation of policies and procedures is essential for all organizations. It is also important to document all observations, incidents, and concerns.

Documentation of Incidents, Observations, and Responsibilities

A child arrived at one agency's program with several bruises and marks. Fortunately, a staff member observed this and completed one of the forms the agency had developed for noting anything unusual or of concern. After further observations, staff members decided to make a report of child abuse, based on their knowledge of the possible indicators.

As soon as the child's parent was told about the allegation, she

---

countered by accusing the agency of abuse, stating that the bruises were inflicted after the child began attending the program. The agency produced its own documentation (the form developed for noting anything unusual or of concern) as well as a list of possible indicators of abuse that staff members noticed in the child. Charges against the agency were dropped, and a full investigation of the mother began.

Documentation is essential for legal reasons as well. In an article in *Camping Magazine*, titled "What You Should Know About Preventing Legal Liability" (Leuenberger, 1982), the author writes the following regarding crisis situations: "Prepare written reports of each factual detail of the occurrence promptly after the event for later reference. Put in as many details as possible. Your memory will never be fresher than right after an incident happens. Take the names of all witnesses present to include in your report whether or not they say they saw anything. Consider immediate pictures of the scene."

Have Official Report Forms Readily Available

Your state's official child-abuse report form should be readily accessible and familiar to all staff members. As has already been mentioned, staff training might include a session familiarizing employees with the form and how to complete it so that there will be no hesitation on their part if and when they need to use it.

Use an Accident Report Form

Whenever an accident occurs, whether it causes a minor or a major injury, it is important to record the information on a specified form that elicits essential information. Accident report forms should include the name of the injured, the name of the person completing the form, what occurred (in detail), what steps were taken, what treatment was given, who was told, the names of any witnesses, observations on the surroundings, and other pertinent information. A sample accident report form, developed by the American Camping Association, is provided in Appendix J.

Use an Incident Report Form

It is wise to develop a form that assists in total documentation of any incident, unusual behavior, or concern. This form should be general, and its use should be widely encouraged.

This form may be different from the accident report form, in that it is to cite noninjurious events or personal observations. Injuries that a child received before or outside of his or her involvement in your organization could also be recorded on this form. A child who becomes unusually angry, a normally outgoing child who becomes withdrawn, a child with an unexplained burn on his or her hand, are examples of incidents that could be recorded but that would not in themselves require making a report of abuse. Appendix K presents an example of an incident report form.

Develop Supplemental Abuse Report Forms

In addition to each state's reporting form, it is beneficial for organizations working with minors to develop supplemental forms. One of these forms might be very similar to the incident report form but specifically designed for reporting suspected child abuse. An example of such a form is provided in Appendix L.

Another useful supplemental form could be an illustration of injuries. Appendix M includes a supplement for indicating where injuries are located.

Use the Checklist of Possible Indicators of Child Abuse

Some organizations may find it helpful to use the possible indicators of abuse given in chapter five as a checklist. This list can be used separately or in conjunction with an incident report form. On this form, the staff member simply checks behaviors that he or she observed in the child. As was cautioned previously, indicators in themselves do not signify abuse, but each must be viewed as being a piece in a puzzle that may end up being abuse.

Some agencies prefer having a form for each participant. Therefore, whenever staff members want to make note of something, they write it on the sheet pertaining to that participant. This system makes it easier to identify concerns, patterns, and potential abuse, because all observations are listed together.

Take Photographs if Possible

When the situation involves an accident or physical abuse with visible injuries, it is to your benefit to photograph the wounds. It is important, however, to know the laws of your particular state pertaining to taking evidence pictures. Be sure to have the consent of the child or of the parent or guardian.

Although the child-abuse authorities generally follow such procedures, you might want a record of the incident for your own records, especially if some time will lapse before officials arrive. Take care, however, to be sensitive to the needs, concerns, and feelings of the child. Here are a few guidelines:

1. Take time to build rapport with the child and to make him or her feel comfortable and relaxed.
2. Photographs should be taken as soon as possible. The first consideration is to get a good picture, regardless of the quality of the camera.
3. If possible, it is best to use a camera that makes images on a negative, so that the images can be enlarged and reproduced, if necessary. A Polaroid camera, for example, makes images that cannot be reproduced.
4. If possible, use a telephoto lens. Such a lens permits you to take close-up shots without intimidating the individual.
5. The most critical consideration in taking pictures is lighting. Make sure that there is adequate lighting with little or no shadows. (Color photographs taken under fluorescent lights can be ruled inadmissible in court, so it is best to turn them off and instead use a flash or some other form of lighting.)
6. Try to have a solid background free of clutter.
7. Do not take pictures solely of the injuries, but include a sequence. For example, with a facial injury, take pictures of the whole child, the head, and several of the

injured cheek, as well as of the possible cause or weapon, if available (belt, branch, canoe paddle, baseball bat).

8. Be sure to label and carefully store the photos.

Use an Initial Health Screening Form

Some organizations conduct a health screening of each child upon arrival. This is especially beneficial for ongoing programs in which children participate on a regular basis or are involved on a residential basis. The health screening form (Appendix O) allows for the identification of any physical concerns or problems that occurred before the child's involvement in the program. By using such a form, an agency can dispel any accusations that the child sustained injuries during his or her participation in the agency's activities.

Use Mandated Reporter Acknowledgment Form

As mentioned in chapter six, in some states each employee considered to be a mandated reporter must acknowledge his or her awareness of child-abuse reporting responsibilities and requirements. Although this is not required in all states, its use is recommended for all agencies. Each mandated reporter signs the form, which includes a summary of the state law and the procedures to be followed. A sample mandated reporter acknowledgment form is included in Appendix A.

Maintain Accurate and Organized Files

Employer, employee, and participant files must be accurate and current. Many patterns leading to suspicion of abuse can be detected through this filing process. Information on each minor in your program should be updated regularly, especially with regard to emergency contacts and phone numbers. Files also should be kept on each employee, with any changes in address or status noted accordingly.

All the forms discussed in this chapter must be readily accessible for reference as needed. Employees' acknowledgment forms, stating their awareness of the state laws pertaining to child abuse, must be kept on file and updated as new employees join the staff.

Organizations that serve young people seek to provide high-quality, safe, and enjoyable experiences for program participants. In order to do that, an organization must educate its staff about potential negative situations. Each situation will call for its own specifically appropriate response. The challenge, therefore, is not only to identify these responses, but also to prepare for them. Documenting what to do so as to prevent unwanted events, providing written procedures to follow in a crisis situation, and completing proper written reports assist organizations in the quest to provide safe, professional, high-quality programs.

Summary

You play a significant role in the enhancement of children's lives. The nature of your work focuses on helping children enjoy and learn from life. In order to accomplish this, however, you must continually be aware of the potential hazards and problems pertaining to your profession, including child abuse. Therefore, it is important that you be well-informed about child abuse. By reading this book, you have demonstrated a desire to assist in the identification and deterrence of this social ill.

Reminders and Suggestions

1. Remember that you need only *suspect* abuse in order to make a report. You do not have to be the judge and jury, nor must you have personally witnessed an abusive situation. You are mandated to report and liable if you do not.
2. Select and train your staff members carefully and thoroughly.
3. Develop written policies that include procedures for dealing with the occurrence, discovery, and accusation of abuse. Make sure that all staff members know the steps to follow and that they use them.

4. Be a child advocate—that is, believe the child and strive to consider his/her safety foremost.

5. Present a child-abuse prevention training session at your agency or organization, including material presented in chapter fourteen and in Appendix I.

6. Frequently review the possible indicators of abuse so that you become more adept at recognizing the signs.

7. Know your state's reporting laws and requirements.

8. Be sensitive, patient, and helpful to those who have been abused—especially to those who are exhibiting undesirable (i.e., negative or withdrawn) behavior. Review chapters nine and ten.

9. Develop and maintain documentation on all minors under your care in an effort to recognize potential problems and/or abuse.

Your awareness of child abuse and your involvement in preventing it demonstrate your commitment to the safe, healthy development of young people. Whether you are educating children about prevention, deterring potential abusers, or carefully monitoring the activities of participants and staff members, your involvement draws us a step closer to the destruction of the abuse cycle.

PART *IV*

Reference Materials

▶ The forms and lists in this final part are here to
help make your job easier. You have permission to
borrow the ideas from any and all of them. You
have permission to photocopy all of them except
the *Checklist of Possible Indicators of Abuse*, the
Staff Application Form, *Accident/Incident Form*,
and the *Camp Health Record for an Individual at
Camp*. These four forms may be purchased from
the American Camping Association bookstore in
quantities of fifty.

Cited Reference List

Ashmen and Mattocks, 1984. "Preparing for a Crisis Situation." *Journal of Christian Camping* 16(4):6.

Brassard, Germain, and Hart, 1987. *Psychological Maltreatment of Children and Youth.* New York, N.Y.: Pergamon Press.

CAPP (Child Abuse Prevention Program). Training. Santa Cruz, CA.: CAPP.

Child Advocacy Council. "Nationwide Poll on Sexual Abuse." *Child Advocacy Council Newsletter.* Fall 1985:20.

Finkelhor, David, 1984. *Child Sexual Abuse: New Theory and Research.* New York, N.Y.: Free Press.

Finkelhor, David, 1988. *Sexual Abuse in Day Care: A National Study.* Durham, N.H.: University of New Hampshire.

Forward, Susan, 1978. *Betrayal of Innocence.* New York, N.Y.: J.P. Tarcher.

Gil, David G., 1969. "Physical Abuse of Children." *Pediatrics.* 44(suppl.):857–864.

Gil, Eliana, 1988. *Outgrowing the Pain: A Book for and About Adults Abused as Children.* New York, N.Y.: Dell.

Groth, A. Nicholas, 1979. *Men Who Rape: The Psychology of the Offender.* New York, N.Y.: Plenum Press.

Lanning, Kenneth V., 1986. *Child Molesters: A Behavioral Analysis for Law Enforcement Officers Investigating Cases of Child Sexual Exploitation.* Washington, D.C.: National Center for Missing and Exploited Children.

Leuenberger, Jan W., 1982. "What You Should Know About Preventing Legal Liability." *Camping Magazine.* 54(no. 4):38–43.

Massachusetts Department of Social Services, 1985. *Child Protective Services Annual Report.* Boston, MA.: Massachusetts Department of Social Services.

Massachusetts Department of Social Services, 1985. *Child Abuse and Neglect: A Fact Sheet.* Boston, MA.: Massachusetts Department of Social Services.

Massachusetts Department of Social Services, 1985. *Making A Report of Child Abuse or Neglect.* Boston, MA.: Massachusetts Department of Social Services.

Mead, James, 1974 unpublished. *Early Detection of the Battered Child Syndrome.* Canyon Lake, CA.: For Kids Sake.

Russell, Diana E.H., 1983. "The Incidence and Prevalence of Intrafamilial and Extrafamilial Sexual Abuse of Female Children." *International Journal on Child Abuse.* New York, N.Y.: Pergamon Press.

San Francisco Child Abuse Council. *Discipline Versus Abuse.* San Francisco, CA.: San Francisco Child Abuse Council.

San Francisco Child Abuse Council, 1989. *Emotional Maltreatment.* San Francisco, CA.: San Francisco Child Abuse Council.

San Francisco Child Abuse Council, 1989. *Indicators of Child Abuse and Neglect.* San Francisco, CA.: San Francisco Child Abuse Council.

Research, 1978. Chicago, IL.: National Committee for the Prevention of Child Abuse and Neglect.

U.S. Attorney General Office, *Meese Commission on Pornography Report.* 1986. Washington, D.C.

Suggested Reading List

Adams, Caren, and Fay, Jennifer, 1981. *No More Secrets: Protecting Your Child From Sexual Assault.* San Luis Obispo, CA.: Impact Publishers.

Baer, Euan, with Dimmock, Peter, 1988. *Adults Molested as Children: A Survivor's Manual for Women and Men.* Orwell, VT.: Safer Society Press.

Bass, Ellen, and Thornton, Louise, Eds., 1983. *I Never Told Anyone: Writings by Women Survivors of Child Sexual Abuse.* New York, N.Y.: Harper Perennial.

Bass, Ellen, and Davis, Laura, 1988. *The Courage to Heal: A Guide for Women Survivors of Child Sexual Abuse.* New York, N.Y.: Harper & Row.

Cunningham, C., and MacFarlane, K., 1977. *Steps to Healthy Touching.* Mount Dora, FL.: KIDSRIGHTS.

Daugherty, L.B., 1984. *Why Me? Help for Victims of Child Sexual Abuse Even If They Are Adults Now.* Racine, WI.: Mother Courage Press.

Finkelhor, David, 1979. *Sexually Victimized Children.* New York, N.Y.: New York Free Press.

Finkelhor, David, Ed., 1986. *A Sourcebook on Child Sexual Abuse.* Beverly Hills, CA.: Sage Publications.

Forward, S., and Buck, C., 1979. *Betrayal of Innocence: Incest and Its Devastation.* New York, N.Y.: Penguin Books.

Freeman, Laura, 1982. *It's My Body: A Book to Teach Young Children How to Resist Uncomfortable Touch.* Parenting Press.

Garbarino, J., Gutman, E., and Seeley, J.W., 1986. *The Psychologically Battered Child.* San Francisco, CA.: Jossey Bass.

Gil, David, 1979. *Child Abuse and Violence.* AMS Press.

Gil, Eliana M., 1982. *Foster Parenting Abused Children.* Chicago, IL.: National Committee on Child Abuse and Prevention.

Gil, Eliana M., 1984. *Outgrowing the Pain: A Book for and About Adults Abused as Children.* San Francisco, CA.: Launch Press.

Gil, Eliana M., 1991. *The Healing Power of Play: Working With Abused Children.* New York, N.Y.: Guilford Press.

Groth, A. Nicholas, 1979. *Men Who Rape.* New York, N.Y.: Plenum Press.

Hart-Rossi, Janie, 1984. *Protect Your Child From Sexual Abuse: A Parent's Guide.* Parenting Press.

Hunter, M., 1990. *Abused Boys: The Neglected Victims of Sexual Abuse.* Lexington, MA.: Lexington Press.

James, Judy, 1985. *It's Not Your Fault.* Chase Franklin Press.

Kempe, Henry C., and Hefler, Ray E., 1968, 1974, 1980. *The Battered Child.* Chicago, IL.: University of Chicago Press.

Kempe, Ruth S., and Kempe, Henry C., 1984. *The Common Secret: Sexual Abuse of Children and Adolescents.* New York, N.Y.: W.H. Freeman and Co.

Lew, Mike, 1990. *Victims No Longer: Men Recovering From Incest and Other Sexual Child Abuse.* New York, N.Y.: Harper & Row.

Maggio, Elizabeth, and Mead, James, 1983. *Child Abuse and Neglect: An Educator's Handbook on Prevention and Recognition.* Brea, CA.: For Kids Sake.

Mead, James, and Balch, Glenn Jr., 1987. *Child Abuse and the Church: A New Mission.* Costa Mesa, CA.: HDL Publishing Co.

Newberger, Eli H., Ed., 1982. *Child Abuse.* Boston, MA.: Little, Brown and Co.

Newman, Susan, 1985. *Never Say Yes to a Stranger.* New York, N.Y.: Putnam Publishing.

Russell, Diana, 1986. The Secret Trauma: Incest in the Lives of Girls and Women. New York, N.Y.: Basic Books.

Russell, Pamela, 1986. *Do You Have A Secret?* Comp Care Publications.

Sanford, L.T., 1982. *Silent Children: A Book for Parents About Prevention of Child Sexual Abuse.* New York, N.Y.: McGraw-Hill.

Terr, T., 1990. *Too Scared to Cry.* New York, N.Y.: Harper & Row.

Wachter, Oralee, 1983. *No More Secrets.* Boston, MA.: Little, Brown and Co.

Woititz, Janet, 1989. *Healing Your Sexual Self.* Deerfield Beach, FL.: Health Communications.

Appendices

A. Sample Mandated Reporter Acknowledgement Form
B. Sample Child Abuse Law (Massachusetts)
C. Sample Child Abuse Report Form (California)
D. Audio-Visual Resources
E. Organizational and Support-Group Resources
F. Sample Staff Application Forms
G. Sample Authorization to Check Criminal Record
H. Case Histories
I. Child Abuse Prevention Information for Children—
   Prevention List
   Alert List
J. Sample Accident/Incident Report Form
K. Sample Incident Report Form
L. Sample Information Supplement Form for Reporting
M. Sample Visual Supplement Form for Reporting
N. Checklist of Possible Indicators of Abuse
O. Sample Health Screening Forms
P. The Effects of Abuse at Different Developmental Stages
Q. Child Abuse Information—Treatment, Intervention,
   Education

Sample Mandated Reporter Acknowledgement Form

Every state maintains a mandatory child abuse reporting law. Many states further require that all employees who are mandated reporters sign a form acknowledging their awareness of the laws and their accompanying responsibilities. Although there are some differences in the requirements from state to state, all of the laws reflect most of the following basic information.

Note: This is not an official mandated reporter acknowledgment form. It is only a representation of the kinds of things that might appear on an official form. Official mandated reporter acknowledgment forms may be obtained from your local child abuse authorities.

Who Must Report

Those who, by the nature of their employment, have contact with children are mandated reporters. These people include the following:

Medical workers: physicians, surgeons, nurses, dentists, residents, interns, pediatricians, chiropractors, psychologists, psychiatrists.

Public/private workers: employees of public and private schools, child-care personnel, resident and day-camp employees, social workers, peace and probation officers, members of the clergy and other youth ministry practitioners, child-welfare supervisors, certified public personnel.

Commercial film or photographic print processors in specified instances, in some states.

Anyone with reasonable grounds to believe a child is in need of protection. Some states require anyone to report when he or she has reasonable grounds to believe that a child has been or is likely to be abused.

What Must Be Reported

Abuse, neglect, and/or abandonment.
Deliberate physical injury of a child.
Sexual molestation.
Causing or allowing great bodily harm, death, unjustifiable physical
    pain or mental suffering, or danger to health.
Exploitation, child pornography and child prostitution.

How To Report

Report any observations, knowledge or reasonable suspicions of abuse immediately by telephone and in writing within 24–36 hours.

Where To Report

Depending on your state, report the suspected abuse to one of the following authorities:

Police department.
Probation department.
Children's protective services.
Welfare department or health department.
Department of social services.

What To Include on the Report

Name of minor(s).
Address of minor(s).
Extent and nature of injury or molestation.
Name of alleged abuser if known.

What Are the Reporting Responsibilities

1. Employee-Supervisor Relationship: If an employee confers with a supervisor who then files a report, only one report is needed. If the supervisor disagrees, however, the employee with the original knowledge or suspicion must make a report.

2. Confidentiality: Mandated reporters must give their name, whereas volunteer (or non-mandated reporters) may do so anonymously. The mandated reporter's name, however, will be kept confidential unless a court orders the information to be disclosed.

3. Immunity: Legally mandated reporters have immunity when making a report. No reporter can be dismissed, disciplined or harassed for filing a report of suspected child abuse.

4. Liability: Legally mandated reporters can be held criminally liable if they fail to report knowledge or suspicions of abuse.

Acknowledgement

I acknowledge that I am a legally mandated reporter and understand the information and requirements described above. I agree to comply with and fulfill these reporting responsibilities.

Employee's Name (print): _____

Employee's Signature: _____

Job Title: _____ Date: ____/____/____

    I have received an explanation of the policies and procedures established by the agency in which I am employed. _____ Yes _____ No

Sample Child Abuse Law (Massachusetts)

Massachusetts General Laws, Chapter 119

SECTION 51A

Injured children, reports; immunity; privileged communications; penalties; notice of determination.

Mandated Reporters

Any physician, medical intern, hospital personnel engaged in the examination, care or treatment of persons, medical examiner, psychologist, emergency medical technician, dentist, nurse, chiropractor, podiatrist, osteopath, public or private school teacher, educational administrator, guidance or family counselor, day care worker, or any other person paid to care for or work with a child in any public or private facility, or home or program funded by the Commonwealth or licensed pursuant to chapter 28A, which provides day care or residential services to children, probation officer, clerk/ magistrate of a district court, social worker, foster parent, firefighter or police officer, who, in his or her professional capacity shall have reasonable cause to believe that a child under the age of 18 is suffering serious physical or emotional injury resulting from abuse inflicted upon him or her including sexual abuse, or from neglect, including malnutrition, or who is determined to be physically dependent upon an addictive drug at birth, shall immediately report such condition to the Department by oral communication and by making a written report within 48 hours after such oral communication; provided, however, that whenever such person so required to report is a member of the staff of a medical or other public or private institution, school or facility, he shall immediately either notify the Department or notify the person in charge of such institution, school or facility, or that person's designated agent, whereupon such person in charge or his or her said agent shall then become responsible to make the report in the manner required by this section. Any such hospital personnel preparing such report may take, or cause to be taken, photographs of the areas of trauma visible on a child who is the subject of such report without the consent of the child's parents or guardians. All such photographs or copies thereof shall be sent to the Department together with such report. Any such person so required to make such oral or written reports who fails to do so shall be punished by a fine of not more than one thousand dollars.

Information Contained In Reports

Said reports shall contain the names and addresses of the child and his parents or other person responsible for his care, if known; the child's age; the child's sex; the nature and extent of the child's injuries, abuse, maltreatment, or neglect; the circumstances under which the person required to report first became aware of the child's injuries, abuse, maltreatment or neglect; whatever action, if any, was taken to treat, shelter, or otherwise assist the child; the name of the person or persons making such report; and any other information which the person reporting believes might be helpful in establishing the cause of the injuries; the identity of the persons responsible therefore; and such other information as shall be required by the Department.

Death Of A Child

Any person required to report under this section who has reasonable cause to believe that a child has died as a result of any of the conditions listed in said paragraph shall report said death to the Department and to the district attorney for the county in which said death occurred and to the medical examiners as required by section six of chapter 38. Any such person who fails to make such a report shall be punished by a fine of not more than one thousand dollars.

Any Person May Report; Immunity

In addition to those persons required to report pursuant to this section, any other person may make such a report if any such person has reasonable cause to believe that a child is suffering from or has died as a result of such abuse or neglect. No person so required to report shall be liable in any civil or criminal action by reason of such report if it was made in good faith; provided, however, that such person did not perpetrate or inflict said abuse or cause said neglect. Any person making such report who, in the determination of the

Department or the district attorney, may have perpe-
trated or inflicted said abuse or caused said neglect may
be liable in a civil or criminal action.

**Retaliation
Against
Reporters;
Liability**

No employer of those persons required to report pursuant to this section shall discharge, or in any manner dis-
criminate or retaliate against, any person who in good
faith makes such a report, testifies or is about to testify
in any proceeding involving child abuse or neglect. Any
such employer who discharges, discriminates or retali-
ates against such a person shall be liable to such person
for treble damages, costs and attorney's fees.

**Notice of DSS'
Determination**

Within 60 days of the receipt of a report by the Department from any person required to report, the Department shall notify such person, in writing, of its
determination of the nature, extent and cause or causes
of the injuries to the child, and the social services that
the Department intends to provide to the child and his
or her family.

**Privileged
Communications**

Any privilege established by section 135 of chapter 112
or by section 20B of chapter 233, relating to confidential
communications shall not prohibit the filing of a report
pursuant to the provisions of the section or the provisions of section 24.

SECTION 51B

Physically or emotionally injured children; duties of
Department. The Department shall:

Investigations

(1) investigate and evaluate the information reported
under section 51A. Said investigation and evaluation
shall be made within 24 hours if the Department has
reasonable cause to believe the child's health or safety is
in immediate danger from further abuse or neglect and
within seven days for all other such reports. The investigation shall include a home visit at which the child is
viewed, if appropriate, a determination of the nature,
extent and cause or causes of the injuries, the identity
of the person or persons responsible therefore, the name,
age and condition of other children in the same household, an evaluation of the parents and the home environment, and all other pertinent facts or matters. Such
determinations and evaluations shall be in writing;

Evaluations

(2) evaluate the household of the child named in the report and make a written determination of the risk of physical or emotional injury to any other children in the same household;

Custody

(3) take a child into immediate temporary custody if the Department has reasonable cause to believe that the removal of the child is necessary to protect him or her from further abuse or neglect; provided, however, that the Department shall make a written report stating the reasons for such removal; and provided further, that if any child is so taken into custody, the Department must file a petition pursuant to section 24 on the next court day; . . .

Sample Child Abuse Report Form (California)

SUSPECTED CHILD ABUSE REPORT

To Be Completed by Reporting Party
Pursuant to Penal Code Section 11166

A. CASE IDENTI-FICATION		TO BE COMPLETED BY INVESTIGATING CPA
		VICTIM NAME: _____
		REPORT NO./CASE NAME: _____
		DATE OF REPORT: _____

B. REPORTING PARTY

NAME/TITLE

ADDRESS

PHONE ( )	DATE OF REPORT	SIGNATURE OF REPORTING PARTY

C. REPORT SENT TO

☐ POLICE DEPARTMENT ☐ SHERIFF'S OFFICE ☐ COUNTY WELFARE ☐ COUNTY PROBATION

AGENCY	ADDRESS

OFFICIAL CONTACTED	PHONE ( )	DATE/TIME

D. INVOLVED PARTIES

VICTIM

NAME (LAST, FIRST, MIDDLE)	ADDRESS	BIRTHDATE	SEX	RACE

PRESENT LOCATION OF CHILD	PHONE ( )

SIBLINGS

NAME	BIRTHDATE	SEX	RACE	NAME	BIRTHDATE	SEX	RACE
1.				4.			
2.				5.			
3.				6.			

PARENTS

NAME (LAST, FIRST, MIDDLE)	BIRTHDATE	SEX	RACE	NAME (LAST, FIRST, MIDDLE)	BIRTHDATE	SEX	RACE
ADDRESS				ADDRESS			
HOME PHONE ( )	BUSINESS PHONE ( )			HOME PHONE ( )	BUSINESS PHONE ( )		

E. INCIDENT INFORMATION

IF NECESSARY, ATTACH EXTRA SHEET OR OTHER FORM AND CHECK THIS BOX. ☐

1. DATE/TIME OF INCIDENT	PLACE OF INCIDENT	*(CHECK ONE)* ☐ OCCURRED ☐ OBSERVED

IF CHILD WAS IN OUT-OF-HOME CARE AT TIME OF INCIDENT, CHECK TYPE OF CARE:

☐ FAMILY DAY CARE ☐ CHILD CARE CENTER ☐ FOSTER FAMILY HOME ☐ SMALL FAMILY HOME ☐ GROUP HOME OR INSTITUTION

2. TYPE OF ABUSE: *(CHECK ONE OR MORE)* ☐ PHYSICAL ☐ MENTAL ☐ SEXUAL ASSAULT ☐ NEGLECT ☐ OTHER

3. NARRATIVE DESCRIPTION:

4. SUMMARIZE WHAT THE ABUSED CHILD OR PERSON ACCOMPANYING THE CHILD SAID HAPPENED:

5. EXPLAIN KNOWN HISTORY OF SIMILAR INCIDENT(S) FOR THIS CHILD:

SS 8572 (REV. 7/87)   ***INSTRUCTIONS AND DISTRIBUTION ON REVERSE***

DO NOT submit a copy of this form to the Department of Justice (DOJ). A CPA is required under Penal Code Section 11169 to submit to DOJ a Child Abuse Investigation Report Form SS-8583 if (1) an active investigation has been conducted and (2) the incident is **not** unfounded.

Police or Sheriff-WHITE Copy; County Welfare or Probation-BLUE Copy; District Attorney-GREEN Copy; Reporting Party-YELLOW Copy

SUSPECTED CHILD ABUSE REPORT
DEPARTMENT OF JUSTICE FORM SS 8572
(REQUIRED UNDER PENAL CODE SECTIONS 11166 AND 11168)

I. REPORTING RESPONSIBILITIES

- No child care custodian or health practitioner reporting a suspected instance of child abuse shall be civilly or criminally liable for any report required or authorized by this article (California Penal Code Article 2.5). Any other person reporting a suspected instance of child abuse shall not incur civil or criminal liability as a result of any report authorized by this section unless it can be proved that a false report was made and the person knew or should have known that the report was false.

- Any child care custodian, health practioner, or employee of a child protective agency (CPA) who has knowledge of or observes a child in his or her professional capacity or within the scope of his or her employment whom he or she reasonably suspects has been the victim of child abuse shall report such suspected instance of child abuse to a child protective agency immediately or as soon as practically possible by telephone and shall prepare and send a written report thereof *within 36 hours* of receiving the information concerning the incident.

- Any child care custodian, health practitioner, or employee of a child protective agency who has knowledge of or who reasonably suspects that mental suffering has been inflicted on a child or its emotional well-being is endangered in any other way, may report such suspected instance of child abuse to a child protective agency. Infliction of willful and unjustifiable mental suffering must be reported.

II. DEFINITIONS

- "Child care custodian" means a teacher, administrative officer, supervisor of child welfare and attendance, or certificated pupil personnel employee of any public or private school; an administrator of a public or private day camp; a licensee, an administrator, or an employee of a community care facility licensed to care for children; headstart teacher; a licensing worker or licensing evaluator; public assistance worker; an employee of a child care institution including, but not limited to, foster parents, group home personnel and personnel or residential care facilities; a social worker or a probation officer or any person who is an administrator or presenter of, or a counselor in, a child abuse presentation program in any public or private school.

- "Health practitioner" means a physician and surgeon, psychiatrist, psychologist, dentist, resident, intern, podiatrist, chiropractor, licensed nurse, dental hygienist, marriage, family, and child counselor, or any other person who is currently licensed under Division 2 (commencing with Section 500) of the Business and Professions Code, any emergency medical technician I or II, paramedic, a person certified pursuant to Division 2.5 (commencing with Section 1797) of the Health and Safety Code, a psychological assistant registered pursuant to Section 2913 of the Business and Professions Code, a marriage, family and child counselor trainee, as defined in subdivision (c) of Section 4980.03 of the Business and Professions Code, an unlicensed marriage, family and child counselor intern registered under Section 4980.44 of the Business and Professions Code, a state or county public health employee who treats a minor for venereal disease or any other condition, a coroner, or a religious practitioner who diagnoses, examines, or treats children.

- "Child protective agency" (CPA) means a police or sheriff's department, a county probation department, or a county welfare department.

III. INSTRUCTIONS

(Section A to be completed by investigating child protective agency)
SECTION A - "CASE IDENTIFICATION": Enter the victim name, report number or case name, and date of report.

(Sections B through E are to be completed by reporting party)
SECTION B - "REPORTING PARTY": Enter your name/title, address, phone number, date of report, and signature.

SECTION C - "REPORT SENT TO": (1) Check the appropriate box to indicate which CPA this report is being sent; (2) Enter the name and address of the CPA to which this report is being sent; and (3) Enter the name of the official contacted at the CPA, phone number, and the date/time contacted.

SECTION D - "INVOLVED PARTIES":

a. VICTIM: Enter the name, address, physical data, present location, and phone number where victim is located (attach additional sheets if multiple victims).

b. SIBLINGS: Enter the name and physical data of siblings living in the same household as the victim.

c. PARENTS: Enter the names, physical data, addresses, and phone numbers of father/stepfather and mother/stepmother.

SECTION E - "INCIDENT INFORMATION": (1) Enter the date/time and place the incident occurred or was observed, and check the appropriate boxes; (2) Check the type of abuse; (3) Describe injury or sexual assault (where appropriate, attach Medical Report - Suspected Child Abuse Form DOJ 900 or any other form desired); (4) Summarize what the child or person accompanying the child said happened; and (5) Explain any known prior incidents involving the victim.

IV. DISTRIBUTION

A. Reporting Party: Complete Suspected Child Abuse Report Form SS 8572. Retain yellow copy for your records and submit top three copies to a child protective agency.

B. Investigating Child Protective Agency: Upon receipt of Form SS 8572, *within 36 hours* send white copy to police or sheriff, blue copy to county welfare or probation, and green copy to district attorney.

90 90347

Audio-Visual Resources

A Chain to be Broken
FMS Production, Inc.
1040 N. Las Palmas Ave.
Los Angeles, CA. 90038
(213) 461-4567

This video includes information, definitions, and insight into both active and passive forms of abuse. Recovering abusers punctuate the message with their own experience. Alcohol, drugs, and today's pressure-charged lifestyles are woven into the picture.

Better Safe Than Sorry, Better Safe Than Sorry II, and Better Safe Than Sorry III
Film Fair Communications
10900 Ventura Blvd.
Studio City, CA. 91604

Better Safe Than Sorry stresses the use of good judgment for children 9–14 years of age as different situations are presented and the viewers are challenged to come up with workable ways to handle each problem. This video encourages children to assume some responsibility for their own safety.

Better Safe Than Sorry II, using a group of children 5–9 years old and TV personality Stephanie Edwards, discusses three simple rules which can help children prevent and/or deal with potential sexual abuse.

Better Safe Than Sorry III is a pre-vention film for adolescents and teens with a special section dealing with boys as victims.

Last Taboo
MTI Teleprograms, Inc.
3710 Commercial Ave.
Northbrook, IL. 60062

This is an intense and dramatic video which shows specialized therapy sessions with adult women who were sexually abused as children.

Sexual Abuse of Children: America's Secret Shame
Aims Instructional Media Services, Inc.
626 Justin Ave.
Glendale, CA. 91201

This video is a realistic presentation of the molestation problem today and includes interviews with molesters and victims.

Shatter the Silence
SL Film Productions
P.O. Box 41108
Los Angeles, CA. 90041
(213) 254-8528

This presents the story of father-daughter incest and is recommended for high school presentations.

170

Child Abuse Today and **Wound Identification**
For Kids Sake, Inc.
P.O. Box 313
Lake Elsinore, CA. 92331-0313
(714) 244-9001

The video, *Child Abuse Today* presents 45 minutes of practical information about child abuse today. *Wound Identification* is a graphic and detailed slide cassette training program for all professionals investigating child abuse.

Acquaintance Rape Prevention Series and **No More Secrets**
ODN Productions
74 Varick St.
New York, N.Y. 10013
(212) 431-8923

The four eight-minute films of the *Acquaintance Rape Prevention Series* examine situations that can lead to acquaintance rape and depicts a teenage girl preventing a potential assault.
No More Secrets is a 13-minute prevention film for children which partially utilizes animation.

Breaking Silence
Future Educational Films, Berkeley, CA
Film Distribution Center
1028 Industry Dr.
Seattle, WA. 98188
(206) 575-1575

This 58-minute documentary uses interviews with therapists and adult survivors of incest.

Child Sexual Abuse: What Your Children Should Know
WTTW, Chicago
Indiana University Audio-Visual Center
Bloomington, IN. 47405

This is a five-part series, each focusing on a particular age group, for children and adults.

Incest: The Victim Nobody Believes
Judge Baker Guidance Center
295 Longwood Ave.
Boston, MA. 02115
(617) 232-8390

This 20-minute film presents a discussion among three young incest survivors.

Crime of Silence: The Sexual Abuse of Children
National Public Radio Publishing
2025 M Street N.W.
Washington, D.C. 20036
(202) 822-2000

This four-part, 30-minutes-each audio cassette includes information on the family, myths of abuse, revealing the abuse, and education and prevention of abuse.

The following are available through:
Simon and Schuster Communications
108 Wilmot
Deerfield, IL. 60015
(800) 621-7870

Childhood Sexual Abuse: Four Case Studies
Cavalcade Productions

This 50-minute presentation includes information appropriate for in-service training in the area of childhood sexual abuse.

Some Secrets Should Be Told
Family Information Systems

In this 12-minute video, a puppeteer helps children understand sexual abuse and what they can do about it.

The Touching Problem
KVOS-TV, Bellingham, WA., and Coalition for Child Advocacy

This docu-drama, geared for children, gives an overview of the child abuse problem and skills for prevention.

Organizational and Support-Group Resources

For Kid's Sake, Inc.
P.O. Box 313
Lake Elsinore, CA. 92331-0313
(714) 244-9001

Canadian Society for the Prevention
    of Cruelty to Children
356 First St., Box 700
Midland, Ontario L4R 9Z9

Childhelp National Child Abuse
    Hotline
(800) 422-4453 or (800) 4-A-CHILD

Covenant House
Toronto, Ontario
(416) 593-4849

National Center for Missing and
    Exploited Children
1835 K St. N.W. Suite 600/700
Washington, D.C. 20006
(202) 634-9821
(800) 843-5678

National Center on Child Abuse and
    Neglect
U.S. Department of Health and
    Human Services
P.O. Box 1182
Washington, D.C. 20013
(703) 385-7565

National Resource Center on Child
    Sexual Abuse
Chesapeake Institute
11141 Georgia Ave., Suite 310
Wheaton, MD. 20902
(800) KIDS 006

National Committee for Prevention of
    Child Abuse and Neglect
332 S. Michigan Ave., Suite 1250
Chicago, IL. 60604-4357
(312) 663-3520

Parents Anonymous, National Office
22330 Hawthorne Blvd., Suite 208
Torrance, CA. 90505
Toll Free (in California)
    (800) 352-0386

Parents United, Inc.; Daughters &
    Sons United; Adults Molested as
    Children United
P.O. Box 952
San Jose, CA. 95108
(408) 280-5055

American Humane Association—
    Children's Division
American Association for Protecting
    Children
9725 W. Hampton
Denver, CO. 80231
(303) 695-0811

Henry Kempe National Center for
    Child Abuse
1205 Oneida St.
Denver, CO. 80220
(303) 321-3963

Society's League Against Molesters
    (SLAM)
524 S. First Ave.
Arcadia, CA. 91006
(818) 445-0802

Child Welfare League of America
1346 Connecticut Ave. N.W.
Washington, D.C. 20036
(202) 833-2850

Royal Family Kids Camp
1068 Salinas Ave.
Costa Mesa, CA. 92626
(714) 556-1420

Sample Staff Application

Camp Staff Application   Form FM 10
Developed by American Camping Association

Return to:

(Please type or print)   Date of Application _____

Name _____   Social Security Number _____

Permanent Address _____   Phone_____
         Street & Number   *City*   *State*   *Zip*   *Area/Number*

School or Business Address_____   Phone_____
              Street & Number   *City*   *State*   *Zip*   *Area/Number*

Are there any reasons you may have difficulty in performing any of the essential elements of the job for which you have applied?   ❑ Yes ❑ No   If so, please explain_____

_____
_____
_____

If you are hired would you desire or need housing for any person(s) other than yourself at the camp?   ❑ Yes ❑ No

Education

Years	School	Major Subjects	Degree Granted

Past Employment *(List previous two summers or years.)*

Dates	Employer	Address/Phone	Nature of Work	Supervisor	Reason for Leaving

Indicate any employer you do not wish us to contact and the reason _____

_____

Camp Experience

Dates	Camp	Director	Address	Camper or Staff

References *(Give names/addresses of 3 persons [not relatives] having knowledge of your character, experience and ability.)*

Name	Address & City	Phone

What type of position do you want at camp? _____   Salary desired?_____

Dates available   From_____   To _____

American Camping Association®

In the following list, put numeral "1" before those activities you can organize and teach as an expert; "2" for those activities in which you can assist in teaching; and, "3" for those which are just your hobby.

Adventure/Challenge
____ Climbing/Rappelling
____ Ropes Course
____ Spelunking

Arts and Crafts
____ Basketry
____ Ceramics
____ Electronics
____ Ham Radio
____ Jewelry
____ Leather Work
____ Macrame
____ Metal Work
____ Model Rocketry
____ Nature Crafts
____ Newspaper
____ Painting
____ Photography
____ Darkroom
____ Sketching
____ Weaving
____ Woodworking

Camp Craft/Pioneering
____ Campcraft
____ OLS Program Leader
____ OLS Instructor
____ Hiking
____ Orienteering
____ Outdoor Cooking
____ Overnight
____ Mountaineering
____ Min.-Impact Camping

Dancing
____ Ballet
____ Folk
____ Social
____ Square
____ Tap
____ _____
____ _____

Dramatics
____ Creative
____ Play Directing
____ Skits and Stunts

Music
____ Lead Singing
____ Instruments (list)
____ Accordion
____ Bugle
____ Piano
____ Guitar
____ _____
____ _____

Nature
____ Animals
____ Astronomy
____ Birds
____ Conservation
____ Flowers
____ Forestry
____ Insects
____ Rocks and Minerals
____ Trees and Shrubs
____ Weather
____ Gardening
____ Animal Care

Sports
____ Archery
____ Archery Certification
____ Badminton
____ Baseball
____ Basketball
____ Boxing
____ Fencing
____ Fishing
____ Bait Casting
____ Fly Casting
____ Hockey
____ Informal Games
____ Ping Pong
____ Riding
____ CHA Certification
____ HSI Instructor
____ Riflery
____ NRA Instructor
____ Soccer
____ Softball
____ Tennis

Track and Field
____ Volleyball
____ Wrestling

Waterfront Activities
____ Canoeing/Kayaking
____ Diving
____ ARC/WSI
____ ARC/EWS
____ BSA/Aquatic Instructor
____ ARC/Lifeguard Training
____ BSA/Lifeguard
____ YMCA/Life Guard
____ Rowing
____ Sailing
____ Scuba
____ Swimming
____ Water Skiing
____ Board Sailing
____ Rafting
____ Synchronized Swimming

Miscellaneous
____ Standard First Aid Cert.
____ Advanced First Aid Cert.
____ Auto Mechanics
____ CPR
____ Campfire Programs
____ Carpentry
____ Electrical
____ Evening Programs
____ Farming
____ First Aid
____ Library
____ Plumbing
____ Shorthand
____ Storytelling
____ Word Processing
____ Worship Services
____ Language

Do you drive? ☐ Yes ☐ No   Valid driver's license? ☐ Yes ☐ No   State_____

Do you have current chauffeur's-type license? ☐ Yes ☐ No

What contributions do you think you can make at camp? _____
_____
_____
_____

What contribution do you think a well-run camp can make to children?_____
_____
_____
_____

Write a brief biographical sketch, including specialized training in camping, and experience or training in other fields which might have a bearing on the position(s) for which you are applying. _____
_____
_____
_____

Are you available for an interview? ☐ Yes ☐ No   Where? _____

I authorize investigation of all statements herein and release the camp and all others from liability in connection with same. I understand that, if employed, I will be an at-will employee and that any agreement to the contrary must be in writing and signed by the director of the camp. I also understand that untrue, misleading, or omitted information herein may result in dismissal, regardless of the time of discovery by the camp.

Signature _____

All statements become part of any future employee personnel files.

This form has been drafted to comply with federal employment laws; however, ACA assumes no responsibility or liability for the use of this form.

Sample Authorization to Check Criminal Record

I, _____ (name) hereby authorize

_____ (name of agency/organization) to obtain information pertaining to any charges and/or convictions I may have had for federal and state criminal law violations. This information will include but not be limited to allegations and convictions for crimes committed upon minors and will be gathered from any law-enforcement agency of this state or any state or federal government, to the extent permitted by state and federal law.

Signed: _____ Date: ____/____/____

Social Security or Identification Number: _____

Driver's License Number: _____

State of Issuance: _____ Expiration Date: ____/____/____

Name of Agency: _____

Authorized Agency Supervisor: _____

Case Histories

Debbie

Debbie's grandfather gave her candy whenever she played certain little games with him. She was instructed not to tell anyone about their fun. As she grew older she began to feel more and more uncomfortable with his little games and asked him to stop. He continued, against her wishes, and insisted that she wasn't to tell anyone. After several years, she finally told her parents. The games stopped, at least with the grandfather, but soon began with her father.

The sexual activities her father asked her to perform became increasingly painful emotionally and physically. He said that he loved her and would have to go to jail if she told. He also placed on her the family's burden by saying, "If you tell, the whole family will fall apart and it would be your fault." As a result, she put up with the abuse for several years before deciding to break the silence. Unfortunately, when Debbie did tell, the family did 'fall apart' and her mother began to resent her.

Bobby

Bobby was three years old and lived with his mother after his parents divorced. His father had visitation rights every other weekend. One weekend when he returned from a visit with his father Bobby had seventeen welts on his buttocks and the back of his thighs. The father told the mother the child fell and hit a coffee table. The mother feared the child had been abused and told her attorney in order to change the father's right to visit the child. The father and mother agreed to have the injury evaluated at a child-abuse center. When asked how the child received seventeen welts by falling against a coffee table just once, the father slowly said there must have been some books on the coffee table which caused the marks.

Later, during play therapy, Bobby reacted normally until it was time to go home. As he went to put the dolls to bed, first placing the girl doll carefully in bed, he picked up the boy doll and beat it with a miniature baseball bat. when asked why he was doing this, Bobby answered, "The baby won't go to bed. It's afraid of the dark." Bobby's acting out demonstrated what had happened to him and why.

Karen

George's sister Karen was older but retarded. They played together, but George resented the special treatment that Karen received. When they played, he would bite and scratch her. Their mother wanted them to play together so that she could have some rest from having to care for Karen 24 hours a day, so she ignored George's roughness. He even began putting her on the sidewalk and running over her with his bicycle. Karen's abuse was detected at her special school and reported. The mother's statement, when asked about the injuries was, "I think it's nice they play together."

Mike

Mike's parents did not really want him because of their busy party schedule. Both parents worked, earned good money and had good health insurance. They took little time to wash or feed Mike and rarely, if ever, held him. They kept him in a plastic infant seat behind a chair in the living room most of the time so he wouldn't be in the way.

Alice

Alice was thirteen when she called the hotline. She asked the counselor what she should do. She had told her mother that she was pregnant and that her father did it. The mother went into a rage, calling the daughter a slut and kicking her out of the house. Alice was picked up by hotline volunteers and brought in for counseling. She was frightened about her future and about what would happen to her family. She wanted her father to stop doing that to her, but she didn't want to report him to the police.

Tom

Tom's father was tired when he came home from work. He ordered his wife to put the crying baby in the closet so the crying would not bother him. Tom was discovered in the closet three days later by a policeman investigating a burglary.

Samantha

When Samantha's older brother reached puberty, he decided to experiment on her with his developing sexuality. He threatened her with physical harm and with the death of her beloved pet if she told or did not comply with his sexual wishes. Samantha didn't reveal the abuse until she was in counseling as an adult.

Jane

It wasn't until Jane went away to college that she realized that her home life was not normal. Throughout her elementary and high school years she slept in bed with her father while her mother had a separate room. Although she reported not having intercourse, she said that touching and fondling were common.

Child Abuse Prevention Information for Children—Prevention List

How to Protect Yourself

Know your full name, address, telephone number (with area code), school name, and telephone numbers of relatives or friends.

Know how to use a telephone to get emergency help.

Tell your parents or guardians where you are going, who you will be with, and when you will return. Always call if you will be late.

Become familiar with the neighborhood and remember specific places to go in case of an emergency (i.e. store, friend's house, gas station, local police, etc.)

If you walk to school, walk with friends and don't hang out in or by deserted buildings, vacant lots or dark alleys.

Play in open areas.

Be careful in public restrooms and don't hang out there. If someone or something seems suspicious, you should leave immediately.

Lock your doors and windows and never let strangers know that you are home alone if they call or come to the door.

Stay in a group when you are on outings. If you get separated, you should wait for the group in an area where there is someone in charge or in an open area where there are lots of people.

Never hitchhike or accept rides in cars when strangers ask directions or offer you presents. Never get in a car, even with people you know, unless your parents or guardians have told you it's okay.

Tell parents, school authorities, or police, about anyone who approaches you, attempts to expose his/her private parts or your private parts. Only parents, doctors or nurses should be allowed to touch your body in a personal manner. If a stranger, relative, friend, or even a parent, doctor or nurse tries to touch you in an uncomfortable way, you should get away quickly. You should never keep things like this a secret.

Ask your parents about sex because they are better informed than school-age friends. You should feel confident enough to tell parents or guardians about confusing or disturbing incidents.

Be alert to the fact that there are people who may want to take advantage of you; that they may tempt you with gifts, candy, and offers of friendship. You should learn to tell the difference between good relationships and relationships that may lead to sexual abuse.

Adapted by permission from San Francisco Child Abuse Council.

Child Abuse Prevention Information for Children—Alert List

You should alert a trusted adult if you encounter someone who:

1. Treats you differently from other children.
2. Wants to spend time alone with you, makes excuses to take you places, or has others leave so you can be alone.
3. Asks you to do things that involve physical contact like giving back rubs or washing your back.
4. Does things to you that involve physical contact like giving back rubs, massaging, or wanting to help you wash.
5. Accidentally-on-purpose touches your private parts— brushes against your breasts while wrestling, or rubs their body against yours.
6. Looks at or touches your body and says it is an inspection to see how you are developing.
7. Puts lotion or ointment on when your mother or others are not around or when nothing is wrong, or asks to put on suntan lotion.
8. Accidentally-on-purpose comes in your room while he/she is undressed, comes in the bathroom when you are there, or lets his/her robe fall open while he/she is walking around.
9. Does not respect your privacy, comes in your room without knocking, does not allow you to close the doors to your bedroom or to the bathroom.
10. Asks questions or makes accusations about sexual things between you and boyfriends or girlfriends.
11. Teaches sex education by showing pornographic pictures, shows his/her body or touches yours.
12. Says things about your body or how you dress that make you uncomfortable.
13. Talks to you about sexual things he/she has done.
14. Tells you private things about his wife or mother or her husband or father.
15. Says you are special, different, the only one who really understands—better than his wife/her husband.
16. Treats you like an adult and/or acts like a kid him/herself.
17. Gives you special privileges or favors and makes you feel like you should return a favor by doing something he/she wants.

18. Treats you meaner than others.
19. Does not let you have friends or do things that other kids your age do.
20. Tells you not to tell anyone about things that happen between you.
21. Comes into your bed.

Source unknown.

Sample Accident/Incident Report Form

Accident/Incident Report Form FM 01

Developed by American Camping Association, Inc.

Camp Name _____ Date _____

Address _____
         Street & Number   *City*   *State*   *Zip*

Name of Injured _____ Age _____ Sex _____ ☐ Camper ☐ Staff ☐ Visitor
               Last   *First*   *Middle*

Address _____ Phone _____
         Street & Number   *City*   *State*   *Zip*   *Area/Number*

Name of Parent/Guardian *(if minor)* _____

Address _____ Phone _____
         Street & Number   *City*   *State*   *Zip*   *Area/Number*

Name/Addresses of Witnesses *(Attach signed statements as to incident.)*

1. _____

2. _____

3. _____

Date of Accident _____ Hour _____ ☐ a.m. ☐ p.m.
                 Day of Week   *Month*   *Day*   *Year*

Describe accident in detail including what the injured person was doing at the time_____

_____

_____

_____

_____

_____

_____

Where occurred? *(Specify location, including location of injured and witnesses. Use diagram to locate persons/objects.)*

Was injured participating in an activity at time of injury? ☐ Yes ☐ No If so, what activity? _____

Any equipment involved in accident? ☐ Yes ☐ No   If so, what kind? _____

What could the injured have done to prevent injury? _____

_____

Emergency procedures followed at time of accident _____

_____

_____

By whom?_____

Submitted by _____ Position _____ Date _____

Copyright 1983 by American Camping Association, Inc. Revised 1990   *American Camping Association*

Medical Report of Accident

Were parents notified? ❑ Yes ❑ No   By ❑ Writing ❑ Phone ❑ Other_____

By whom?_____ Title _____ When _____
                                                                                                        Time   Date

Parent's Response _____

_____

Where was treatment given?   ❑ At Accident Site ❑ Camp Health Service ❑ Doctor's Office ❑ Hospital

If treatment was given at camp, where?_____

   By whom? _____ Date _____

   Treatment given_____

   Was injured retained overnight in camp health service? ❑ Yes ❑ No   If so, when?_____

   Treatment given _____

   By Whom? _____ Title _____

   Date released from health service _____

   Released to   ❑ Camp Activities ❑ Home ❑ Other _____

Treatment given elsewhere than camp? ❑ Yes ❑ No   Where? _____

   By whom? _____ Date _____

   Was injured retained overnight in hospital? ❑ Yes ❑ No   If so, which? _____

   Where?_____ Date _____ ❑ Out-patient ❑ In-patient

   Name of physician in attendance_____

   Date released from hospital _____

   Released to   ❑ Camp ❑ Health Service ❑ Home ❑ Other _____

Comments _____

_____

_____

Persons notified such as camp owner/sponsor, board of directors, etc.

Name	Position	Date
_____	_____	_____
_____	_____	_____
_____	_____	_____

Describe any contact made with/by the media regarding this situation _____

_____

Signed _____ Position _____ Date _____

Insurance Notification   Date

1. ❑ Parent's Insurance   By ❑ Parent ❑ Camp   _____
2. ❑ Camp Health Insurance   _____
3. ❑ Worker's Compensation   _____
4. ❑ Camp Liability Insurance   _____

186

Sample Incident Report Form

Date: ____/____/____

Name of Person Reporting: _____

Title/Work Responsibilities: _____

1. Briefly state (in a few words) the nature of the incident (i.e. fight, argument, tantrum, discipline action, unusual reaction).

2. List the names, age, and sex of those involved in the incident.

   a.) Name: _____ Age: _____ Sex: M F

   b.) Name: _____ Age: _____ Sex: M F

   c.) Name: _____ Age: _____ Sex: M F

   d.) Name: _____ Age: _____ Sex: M F

   e.) Name: _____ Age: _____ Sex: M F

3. When did the incident occur? Date: ____/____/____ Time: _____
4. At what location did the incident occur?

5. Explain what happened prior to the incident.

6. Explain what happened during the incident.

7. Explain what happened following the incident.

8. Additional comments/concerns/observations. Use the back side if necessary.

Signature: _____ Received by: _____

Sample Information Supplement Form for Reporting

1. About the child/youth

    Name: _____

    Age: _____   Birth Date: ___/___/___   Sex: M F

    Home Address: _____

    _____

    Home Phone: _____ Emergency Phone: _____

    Parent Name(s): Mother _____ Father _____

    Work Phone (Mother) _____

    Work Phone (Father) _____

2. About the person reporting

    Name: _____

3. About the report

    Report called in:

    _____ Yes _____ No Date: ___/___/___ Time: _____

    Name of person to whom report was made: _____

    Title: _____ Agency: _____

    Sent In:

    _____ Yes _____ No Date: ___/___/___ Time: _____

    Where was the report sent? Agency: _____

    Attach a copy of the completed state child-abuse report form.

4. About the alleged perpetrator

    Name: _____

    Address (if known): _____

    _____

    Relation to the minor (i.e. family, baby-sitter, neighbor): _____

5. The report was made as a result of:

    a. _____ Observing physical and/or behavioral indicators which led to the suspicion of abuse.

    b. _____ A statement made by the minor.

       If based on observation, attach the *Checklist of Possible Indicators of Abuse.*

       If based on the minor's statement, write what was said accurately and objectively. Use the back side if needed.

       What were the circumstances surrounding the disclosure? When, where, how did the individual tell you? Use the back side if needed.

6. Additional comments, concerns, or observations. Use the back side if necessary.

7. Signature: _____

   Job Title: _____ Date: ____/____/____

Sample Visual Supplement Form for Reporting

Indicate on the following diagram the areas in which physical injury is evident, using "X" to indicate the location of superficial injuries, "O" to indicate the location of deep injuries and "shaded areas" to indicate areas of apparent burn. Beside each injury or apparent burn, please note the color, size, pattern, texture, and degree of pain.

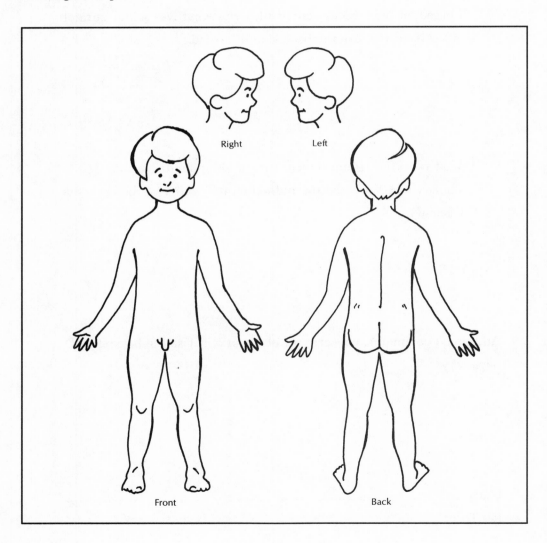

Right   Left

Front   Back

Checklist of Possible Indicators of Abuse

Name: _____ Nickname: _____

Address: _____

_____ Phone Number: _____

Age: ___ Birth Date: ___/___/___ Sex: ____ M ____ F

Parent/Guardian: _____ Relationship: _____

Parent/Guardian: _____ Relationship: _____

Observations: If more than one person utilizes this form, it is beneficial to use different marks. The first person could use check marks (✓), the second pluses (+) and the third zeros (0).

Sexual Abuse— Behavioral Indicators

___ 1. Is reluctant to change clothes in front of others.
___ 2. Is withdrawn.
___ 3. Exhibits unusual sexual behavior and/or knowledge beyond that which is common for his/her developmental stage.
___ 4. Has poor peer relationships.
___ 5. Either avoids or seeks out adults.
___ 6. Is pseudo-mature.
___ 7. Is manipulative.
___ 8. Is self-conscious.
___ 9. Has problems with authority and rules.
___ 10. Exhibits eating disorders.
___ 11. Is self-mutilating.
___ 12. Is obsessively clean.
___ 13. Uses or abuses alcohol and/or other drugs.
___ 14. Exhibits delinquent behavior such as running away from home.
___ 15. Exhibits extreme compliance or defiance.
___ 16. Is fearful or anxious.
___ 17. Exhibits suicidal gestures and/or attempts suicide.
___ 18. Is promiscuous.
___ 19. Engages in fantasy or infantile behavior.
___ 20. Is unwilling to participate in sports activities.
___ 21. Has school difficulties.

Sexual Abuse— Physical Indicators

___ 1. Has pain and/or itching in the genital area.
___ 2. Has bruises or bleeding in the genital area.
___ 3. Has venereal disease.
___ 4. Has swollen private parts.
___ 5. Has difficulty walking or sitting.
___ 6. Has torn, bloody, and/or stained underclothing.
___ 7. Experiences pain when urinating.

___ 8. Is pregnant.

___ 9. Has vaginal or penile discharge.

___ 10. Wets the bed.

Emotional Abuse— Behavioral Indicators

___ 1. Is overly eager to please.

___ 2. Seeks out adult contact.

___ 3. Views abuse as being warranted.

___ 4. Exhibits changes in behavior.

___ 5. Is excessively anxious.

___ 6. Is depressed.

___ 7. Is unwilling to discuss problems.

___ 8. Exhibits aggressive or bizarre behavior.

___ 9. Is withdrawn.

___ 10. Is apathetic.

___ 11. Is passive.

___ 12. Has unprovoked fits of yelling or screaming.

___ 13. Exhibits inconsistent behavior at home and school.

___ 14. Feels responsible for the abuser.

___ 15. Runs away from home.

___ 16. Attempts suicide.

___ 17. Has low self-esteem.

___ 18. Exhibits a gradual impairment of health and/or personality.

___ 19. Has difficulty sustaining relationships.

___ 20. Has unrealistic goal setting.

___ 21. Is impatient.

___ 22. Is unable to communicate or express his/her feelings, needs, or desires.

___ 23. Sabotages his/her chances of success.

___ 24. Lacks self-confidence.

___ 25. Is self-deprecating and has a negative self-image.

Emotional Abuse— Physical Indicators

___ 1. Has a sleep disorder (nightmares or restlessness).

___ 2. Wets the bed.

___ 3. Exhibits developmental lags (stunting of his/her physical, emotional, and/or mental growth).

___ 4. Is hyperactive.

___ 5. Exhibits eating disorders.

Physical Abuse— Behavioral Indicators

___ 1. Is wary of adults.

___ 2. Is either extremely aggressive or withdrawn.

___ 3. Is dependent and indiscriminate in his/her attachments.

___ 4. Is uncomfortable when other children cry.

___ 5. Generally controls his/her own crying.

___ 6. Exhibits a drastic behavior change when not with parents or caregiver.

___ 7. Is manipulative.

___ 8. Has poor self-concept.

___ 9. Exhibits delinquent behavior, such as running away from home.

___ 10. Uses or abuses alcohol and/or other drugs.

___ 11. Is self-mutilating.

___ 12. Is frightened of parents or going home.

___ 13. Is overprotective of or responsible for parents.

___ 14. Exhibits suicidal gestures and/or attempts suicide.

___ 15. Has behavior problems at school.

Physical Abuse— Physical Indicators

___ 1. Has unexplained* bruises or welts, often clustered or in a pattern.

___ 2. Has unexplained* and/or unusual burns (cigarettes, doughnut-shaped, immersion-lines, object-patterned).

___ 3. Has unexplained* bite marks.

___ 4. Has unexplained* fractures or dislocations.

___ 5. Has unexplained* abrasions or lacerations.

___ 6. Wets the bed.

(* Or explanation is inconsistent or improbable.)

Neglect—Behavioral Indicators

___ 1. Is truant or tardy to school often or arrives early and stays late.

___ 2. Begs or steals food.

___ 3. Attempts suicide.

___ 4. Uses or abuses alcohol and/or other drugs.

___ 5. Is extremely dependent or detached.

___ 6. Engages in delinquent behavior, such as prostitution or stealing.

___ 7. Appears to be exhausted.

___ 8. States frequent or continual absence of parent or guardian.

Neglect—Physical Indicators

___ 1. Frequently is dirty, unwashed, hungry, or inappropriately dressed.

___ 2. Engages in dangerous activities (possibly because he/she generally is unsupervised).

___ 3. Is tired and listless.

___ 4. Has unattended physical problems.

___ 5. May appear to be overworked and/or exploited.

Observer #1: _____ Date: ___/___/___

Observer #2: _____ Date: ___/___/___

Observer #3: _____ Date: ___/___/___

Sample Health Screening Forms

Camp Health Record
Individual at Camp   Form FM02

Developed and Approved by
American Camping Association, Inc. with
American Academy of Pediatrics

Camp Name

Name _____ Age _____ Sex _____

Entrance Date _____ Departure Date _____

Examination Entrance By _____	Departure By _____	Important Observations to Follow While at Camp
Height		
Weight		
Temperature		
Eyes		
Nose		
Ears		
Throat		
Teeth		
Posture		
Skin		

Copyright 1983 by ***American Camping Association, Inc.***   Revised 1990   .(over)

Instructions and Report to Parents or Guardian (Health Progress):

_____

_____

_____

Signature_____

Health Record While at Camp (To include date, time, illness, treatment, initials of person treating:)

_____
_____
_____
_____
_____
_____
_____
_____
_____
_____
_____
_____
_____
_____
_____
_____

Camper's Name   Last   First   Initial   *Cabin or Tent*

American Camping Association

Name: _____

Upon Arrival

Person Conducting Health Screen: _____ Date: ____/____/____

1. Weight: _____ Height: _____ Temperature: _____

2. Currently on medication? _____ Yes _____ No

   If Yes, list the medication(s). _____

   _____

   Who will dispense the medication(s)?

   Agency employee _____ Program participant _____

3. Any known physical limitations? _____ Yes _____ No

   If Yes, explain the nature of the limitation (i.e. swimming, running).

4. Any recent exposure to communicable diseases? _____ Yes _____ No

   If Yes, cite which one:

5. Observations—circle and explain those of concern.

   _____ Skin: (bruises, infection, scrapes, injuries) _____

   _____ Posture: (curvature of the spine) _____

   _____ Eyes: (red, pink, drainage, pain) _____

   _____ Ears: (pain, partial hearing, drainage) _____

   _____ Nose: (cold, frequent nosebleeds, drainage) _____

   _____ Throat: (red, cough, sore, hoarse) _____

   _____ Teeth: (pain, loose, cavities, gum irritation) _____

   _____ Hair: (knotted, lice) _____

   _____ Feet: (blisters, sores, fungus) _____

   6. List and explain any observations which are questionable or of concern.

7. Recommendations:

_____ Notify parent/guardian of concern.   _____ Make a child abuse report.

_____ Recommend medical treatment.   _____ Maintain careful observations.

The Effects of Abuse at Different Developmental Stages

The following information lists some of the typical responses of individuals as a result of abuse. This material was provided by the San Francisco Child Abuse Council, which states that "these responses overlap and are not designed to be rigidly applied." Each victim responds to abuse individually and progresses through the developmental stages at varying times, so these are meant to be general guidelines.

Infants and Toddlers

Physical Abuse	Sexual Abuse	Neglect
withdrawal/apathy	sexualized behavior	withdrawal/apathy
aggression	difficulty sleeping	rocking
head-banging	difficulty relaxing	fearfulness
hypervigilance	clinginess	lethargy
anxiety/fearfulness	difficulty eating	failure to thrive
subdued crying	colic	speech and language delays
clinginess	passivity and withdrawal	
poor eye contact	fussiness	
indiscriminate attaching		
inappropriate reactions to pain		

Elementary School Age

Physical Abuse	Sexual Abuse	Neglect
withdrawal/apathy	sexualized behavior	withdrawal/apathy
aggression	inability to relate to peers	fearfulness
self-destructive behavior	seeking/avoiding adults	learned helplessness
attention getting	pseudo-maturity	hoarding food
self-mutilation	manipulative behavior	clinginess or neediness
accident proneness	easily distracted	pseudo-independence

(continued)

Physical Abuse	Sexual Abuse	Neglect
difficulties in school	self-consciousness	regressive behavior
speech/learning problems	eating disorders	thumb sucking
fear of failure	school problems	inappropriate clothing
drug or alcohol abuse	bed-wetting	
running away		
bed-wetting		

Adolescence

Physical Abuse	Sexual Abuse	Neglect
withdrawal/apathy	sexualized behavior	withdrawal/apathy
aggression	acting out	aggression
anti-social behavior	promiscuity/prostitution	eating disorder
poor peer relations	extreme defiance or	inability to keep friends
tough-guy image	compliance	unkempt appearance
desire for adult attention	isolation	drug/alcohol abuse
prostitution	fears/anxiety	
running away	self-mutilation	
drug/alcohol abuse	suicidal gestures	
eating problems	obsessive cleanliness	
difficulties in school	pseudo-maturity	
	eating disorders	
	drug/alcohol abuse	
	delinquent behavior	
	running away	

Adulthood

Physical Abuse	Sexual Abuse	Neglect
inability to form lasting, meaningful, or satisfying relationships	sexual difficulties	relationship difficulties
isolation	problems with intimacy	depression
frequent relocations	shame for their body	drug/alcohol abuse
anger or fear	low self-worth in sexuality	isolation
low self-esteem	inability to assert self	lack of interest in self or others
drug/alcohol abuse	feelings of being victimized	
	drug/alcohol abuse	
	low self-esteem	
	eating disorders	

Child Abuse Information—
Treatment, Intervention, Education

Prevention Through Treatment

Successful treatment may keep an abuser from abusing again, and an abused minor from becoming an abuser, and may protect future generations of the family (or families if they come from different homes). Treatment can be for the offender, for the child and/or for the families, and usually consists of either individual, family, or support-group counseling.

Parents Anonymous is an example of a support group which was developed as an informal network of group therapy programs for persons sharing the mutual desire to get better. Many therapists have also begun what many call "Survivors Groups." In these groups, members with similar experiences get together to help each other work towards being a survivor rather than a victim.

Prevention Through Intervention

Intervention programs aim to avert a tragedy in the midst of a crisis, and to help the individuals through the crisis. Examples of crisis-intervention programs are hotlines staffed by trained volunteers who are available on a twenty-four-hour basis, and infant drop-off centers or crisis nurseries where parents can leave their child or children for a few hours without questions asked. This latter service might also include emergency shelter facilities.

Prevention Through Education

Education for the prevention of child abuse will not be successful unless it reaches all of those involved; the child, the parent, those working with children, and those professionals working with abusive situations. If a child reveals an abusive encounter but it falls on deaf ears, nothing will happen and the child will probably never tell again. If parents fail to believe their child's statement of abuse, well-trained professionals are useless. Everyone involved must be educated about the existence and prevention of abusive situations.

Most physical abuse is a result of parenting frustration. Therefore, training programs have been developed in parenting skills which include such topics as stress reduction and discipline methods. These courses are being offered in high schools, community colleges, hospitals, churches, community centers, and adult-education programs.

Molestation prevention is being taught to pre-school and school-age children as well as adolescents. These programs seek to inform the participants about the need to disclose abuse, what to do if abused, and how to prevent abuse.

Index

A

accident report forms, *144*
accidental injury or physical abuse, *19*
accusations of child abuse, *75–81*
Adams, Caren, *78*
aggressiveness/hostility, *90*
American Camping Association interview
  guidelines, *117–118*
anger, *86*
Ashmen, John, *142*

B

babysitter abuse, *27*
background indicators of child abuse, *31–33*
bed-wetting, *39–40*
behavioral indicators of child abuse
    emotional abuse, *42–43*
    neglect indicators, *41–42*
    physical abuse, *43–44*
    sexual abuse, *40–41*
Bergh, Henry, *14*
Betrayal of Innocence (Forward), *23*
blaming others, *105*
bonding, *34*
bruises, *45, 50*
burns, *49–51*

C

California State Department of Social
  Service, *5*
calmness, *68*
Camp Quaker Heights, *142*
camp staff members, *4*
causes of abuse, *31–37*
    background indicators, *31–33*
    personality factors, *35–37*
    situational factors, *33–35*
child abuse. *See also* specific types of child
  abuse
    accusations, *75–81*
    causes, *31–37*
    checklist, *145–146*
    current, *14–15*
    defined, *17*
    history, *11–15*
    outcomes, *88–92*
    prevalence, *4–5*
    prevention for children, *136–138*
    prevention for parents, *135–136*
    programs, *98–99*
    reporting rate in U.S., *15*
    responses, *6*
    statistics, *4–5, 11–12*
    suspicions, *67–73*
    types, *18–29*
    victims, *93–99*
    what to do and what to report, *67–70*

Child Abuse Prevention Program
  (CAPP), *136–138*
child abuser characteristics, *103–113*
child advocates, *98*
child as non-threatening lover, *113*
child care, lack of experience and education
  in, *32–33*
child-care workers, *4*
Child Molesters: A Behavioral Analysis
  (Lanning), *107*
child pornography, *113*
children testifying, *59–60*
cigarette burns, *50*
closeting, *22*
confidentiality, *67, 97*
contact lists, *142*
cycle of abuse, *15*

D

damaged-goods syndrome, *87*
degradation, *25*
delayed adolescent sexual curiosity, *111–112*
denial, *84*
dependency problems, *89*
dependent abuse, *28–29*
depression, *36–37*
difficulty with boundaries, *91*
direct sexual abuse, *23*
discipline procedures, *132*
discipline versus child abuse, *134–135*
divorce, *26*
documentation, *139–148*
    dealing with parents, *142–143*
    developing policies, *140–141*
    developing procedures, *141–142*
    of incidents, observations, and
      responsibilities, *143–148*
    photographs, *146–147*
    report forms, *144–145*

E

elder abuse, *28–29*
emotional abuse
    abuser characteristics, *106*
    behavioral indicators, *42–43*
    defined, *24–25*
    physical indicators, *43*
environmental deprivation, *21*
exaggerated accusation, *81*
exposure, *22*

F

failure to thrive, *20–21*
false accusations, *79–80*
family violence, *25–26*
Fay, Jennifer, *78*
fear, *85*
Federal Child Abuse Prevention and Treatment
  Act, *17*
feelings about abuse, *85–87*
female sexual offenders, *111–113*
females, sexual abuse of, *5*
filth and infestation, *21*
financial problems, *35*
Finkelhor, David, *5, 23*
fixated pedophiles, *107–108*
fixed-object lacerations, *47*
For Kids Sake, Inc., *5, 45*
Forward, Susan, *23*
fractures, *48, 51*

G

geographic burns and scalding, *49–50*
Gil, Eliana, *83*
glove burns, *49*
guilt, *86*

H

head injuries, *48, 50*
health screen forms, *147*
helplessness/depression, *91*
homosexuality, *89*
hot temper, *105*
housing, poor and/or crowded, *35*

I

immersion burns, *49*
immunity, *58*
imprint of an object on the skin, *47*
incident report form, *145*
indicators of child abuse, *39–51*
indirect sexual abuse, *22*
infanticide, *13*
institutional abuse, *28*
involvement, importance of
    for the child, *6–7*
    for the family, *7–8*
    protection against accusations, *8*
    responsibility, *9*
    state reporting requirements, *8*

202

L

lacerations, *50*
Lanning, Kenneth, *107*
life crisis, *35*
Lloyd, David, *78*
long-bone fractures, *48*
low self-esteem, *90*

M

mandated reporters, *53–54*
 acknowledgment form, *147*
marital/relationship problems, *35*
Massachusetts Department of Social
 Services, *5*
maternal-infant bonding, lack of, *34*
Mattocks, Ron, *142*
media contact, *142*
medical deprivation, *21–22*
medical workers, *54*
Meese Commission on Pornography, *113*
mental abuse, *25*
minimizing, *84*
mother and child for sexual stimulation, *112*
multiple injuries, *45*
multiple-plane injuries, *48*

N

National Child Abuse Hotline, *61*
National Clearinghouse on Family
 Violence, *61*
National Society for the Prevention of Cruelty
 to Children, *14*
negative attitude, *105*
negative behaviors, *97*
neglect, *20*
 behavioral indicators, *41–42*
 physical indicators, *42*
New York Foundling Hospital, *13*
nonreporting penalties, *61*

O

*Outgrowing the Pain: A Book for and About
 Adults Abused as Children* (Gil), *83*
overpunishment, *36*

P

parental stress, *33*
parents, abuse prevention for, *135–136*
pedophiles, *107–111*
penalties for nonreporting, *61*

personality factors, *35–37*
photographs for documentation, *146–147*
physical child abuse, *18–19*
 abuser characteristics, *104–106*
 behavioral indicators, *43–44*
 or accidental injury, *19*
 physical indicators, *44*
 primary target zone, *44–46*
 screening test, *19*
 wound identification, *44–51*
physical indicators
 emotional abuse, *43*
 neglect, *42*
 physical abuse, *44*
 sexual abuse, *41*
physical problems, *90*
poor and/or crowded housing, *35*
poor self-image, *36*
preventing child abuse, *129–131*
prior arrests or convictions, *104*
privacy, *67, 97*
programs for abused, *98–99*
promiscuity, *88*
prostitutes, *112–113*
public/private workers, *54*
pummeling, *47*

R

rationalizing, *84*
reactions to abuse, *83–92*
recanting, *85*
recreational staff, *4*
references from staff applicants, *119–120*
regressed pedophiles, *109*
rejection, *37*
reporting concerns
 abuser arrested, *59*
 child testifying, *59–60*
 confidentiality, *58–59*
 immunity, *58*
 interviewing child, *59*
 lack of solid evidence, *56–57*
 liability for failing to report, *57*
 repeating, *73*
 repercussions for reporting, *58*
 supervisor refuses, *59*
 when report is made, *57–58*
reporting laws, *60–61*
 penalties for nonreporting, *61*
reporting requirements, *53–61*
 acknowledging, *55*

reporting requirements—cont
    state requirements, *8*
    what must be reported, *54–55*
    when to report, *54*
    where to report, *54–55*
rescuing others, *91–92*
responses to child abuse, *6*
ridicule, *25*
role reversal, *37*
Royal Family Kids Camp (RFKC), *98–99*
Russell, Diana, *5*

S

scalding, *49–51*
The Secret Trauma, (Russell), *5*
selective memory, *85*
self-image, poor, *36*
separation and divorce, *26*
series straight-line lacerations, *47*
sex offenders, *107–113*
sexual abuse, *22–24*
    abuser characteristics, *106–107*
    behavioral indicators, *40–41*
    of females, *5*
    physical indicators, *41*
    statistics, *23*
shame, *86–87*
sibling abuse, *26–27*
situational factors of child abuse, *33–35*
skull injuries, *48*
social isolation, *33–34*
Society for the Prevention of Cruelty to
    Animals, *14*
Society for the Prevention of Cruelty to
    Children, *14*
spiral fractures, *48*
spoon trick, *47*
staff, child abuse prevention for, *132–136*
staff selection, *115–120*
    application, *115–116*
    interviewing, *116–119*
    screening for abuser
        characteristics, *103–113*
staff training, *121–128*
    commitment, *122*
    guidelines, *122–123*
    how to present, *127*

staff training—cont
    resources, *128*
    training outlines, *124–127*
    what to present, *123*
    who should present, *122–123*
state reporting requirements, *8*
statistics of child abuse, *4–5, 11–12*
stocking burns, *49*
substitute accusation, *79–80*
supplemental abuse report forms, *145*
suspecting abuse, *65–73*
suspicious or unusual observations, *133*

T

targeted children, *34*
Tomlinson-Keasy, Carol, *78*
tough skin, *90*
transference, *79*
trust problems, *89*

U

unconditional love, *97*
undifferentiated pedophiles, *109–110*
unintentional abuse, *29*
unrealistic expectations, *36*

V

victims
    child abuse, *31, 93–99*
    family violence, *32*
    questions they ask, *87–88*
    substance abuse, *32*

W

welts, *45*
women who molest for profit, *112–113*
wounds
    identification summary, *50–51*
    primary target zone, *44–46*
wraparound injuries, *45, 47*
wrong accusations, *80*

YZ

youth service organizations, *65–67*
zebra burns, *49*